THREE

Forgiveness

God's Redemption in the Dark Places of Addiction

KIMBERLY DEWBERRY

ELECTIO PUBLISHING
first century principles.
a twenty-first century approach.

Three Weeks to Forgiveness: God's Redemption in the Dark Places of Addiction

By Kimberly Dewberry

Copyright 2018 by Kimberly Dewberry. All rights reserved.

Cover Design by eLectio Publishing.

ISBN-13: 978-1-63213-486-8

Published by eLectio Publishing, LLC

Little Elm, Texas

http://www.eLectioPublishing.com

5 4 3 2 1 eLP 22 21 20 19 18

Printed in the United States of America.

The eLectio Publishing creative team is comprised of: Kaitlyn Campbell, Emily Certain, Lori Draft, Court Dudek, Jim Eccles, Sheldon James, and Christine LePorte.

Scripture quotations taken from the New American Standard Bible® (NASB), Copyright © 1960, 1962, 1963, 1968, 1971, 1972, 1973, 1975, 1977, 1995 by The Lockman Foundation. Used by permission. www.Lockman.org.

Publisher's Note

The publisher does not have any control over and does not assume any responsibility for author or third-party websites or their content.

For our heavenly Father,
I thank Him for loving me anyway
and may His glory shine through these pages.

For Patrick,
thank you for your unconditional love
and your unending support.

For Dad,
thank you for the privilege
of getting to be your daughter.

"When you pass through the waters, I will be with you; and through the rivers, they will not overflow you. When you walk through the fire, you will not be scorched; Nor will the flame burn you."

Isaiah 43:2

Contents

Foreword

From a spiritual perspective life is a total paradox: When we attempt to find ourselves apart from God, we only end up losing ourselves. Coming to the end of ourselves is the very thing that has to occur so that we can find our true self in God. Even when we don't yet have a spiritual grid, we set out on that journey to know who it is we are and hoping to find life, peace, and contentment. For many of us, and especially those who grow up in an alcoholic home, this journey originates in the dysfunction of addiction. Attempting to find peace while submerged in a family system of addiction are murky waters to swim in.

God permits these experiences and ultimately uses them to be the very path which could allow us to come to the end of ourselves. Since we can only truly find ourselves in Him, he allows pain so that we will turn to Him. In turning to Him, He can then redeem our life's struggles by finding peace in Him.

Kimberly's story typifies the experience of someone growing up in an alcoholic home that is full of pain and disillusionment. She, like so many of us, attempted to save herself by her strength, only leading to more pain and disappointment. *Three Weeks to Forgiveness* tells the story of how Kimberly came to the end of herself and began depending on God. Her story takes us to the crossroad where living life in our power graciously fails, so we become ready to turn to God in total dependence. You will read how this is the path that leads to God, the only real source of life, freedom, and peace. Kimberly's story will encourage you by seeing how God did not waste her pain, but instead how He used it to lead her to Himself where she found peace and the ability to forgive!

Evan Buja LPC, DMin

Lakepointe Church Counseling Center

Prologue

August 2015

Until late that hot summer, I had never watched someone die. I had never been around anyone dying from cancer. These weeks exposed a power I had only heard or read about but hadn't observed in person. Seeing depictions of death in movies or reading about it in books did nothing to prepare me to witness the decimation of body, spirit, mind, and dignity brought on by the cannibalism of cancer. The trajectory of the months ahead and the people God placed in my life impacted me in ways I couldn't have dreamed. Those days revealed things that laid long buried.

As a teen, Dad taught me how to fight in order to defend myself. His street-learned instinct of fight, *not* flight was drilled into me. The two of us shadowboxed in the living room as he showed me the right moves to ward off a would-be attacker, or in my case, a girl in high school much larger than me. This same mindset influenced his last three weeks on earth, battling with his hospital bed, emesis bags, stomach tube, and wheelchair. The cancer caused severe nausea. Although he craved his favorite foods he couldn't keep any of it down longer than ten to fifteen minutes. His rugged body wasted away to a scrawny frame of bones. His hearing and eyesight failed rapidly. Although he was only sixty-three, he looked like an old man. Gaunt and pale, his eyes clouded over and looked forlorn. The man I remembered from my distant past slowly slipped from me, but not without a fight.

Day one of Dad's last three days proved to be trying. We knew the end of his life on earth drew near. We knew his body was giving out. Time with him was short. We took care of Dad's needs in shifts. I had stayed at his bedside the night before and his restlessness grew more frequent. He could not find the comfort he so desperately craved because of the stiff mattress of the hospital bed, so sleep eluded him. Before the sun shone into his room, he asked me if we could go smoke. During the three weeks he was a guest in my home, smoking in the garage became our exclusive time together. Even though he was dying, we figured as long as he felt like it, smoking was one of life's pleasures we would not force him to do without.

I helped his feeble, unsteady body into the wheelchair, gave him his maroon hat to place on his head, and handed him his vomit bag, towel, and smokes. Off we went to maneuver our way from the hospital bed in my dining room, through the kitchen, and into the solitude of the garage. I situated his chair like I had so many times before, next to the table with the ashtray, and opened the garage door so he could look out into the front yard. He sat quietly enjoying the peaceful morning before the rest of the neighborhood stirred, the cottontail bunnies frolicking around the dew-kissed grass and the sun rising above the house across the street as he puffed on his cigarette. I watched his face and wondered what he was thinking. That morning, as I did occasionally, I asked what was on his mind. He turned his head and looked into my eyes.

"Have I been a good dad to you, Mija?"

I sat for a moment looking at his intense dark brown eyes.

"You don't worry about it. You were a good dad to me," I replied without hesitation. In that moment, I realized how sad he had been inside. Broken. Damaged. Addicted.

"It was a privilege to be your dad." His eyes never left mine as he spoke.

"The privilege was mine," I said, willing the tears not to stream down my face.

I meant what I told him that day. Although there were times growing up when his fathering skills faltered because of the addiction, there were many other times when his love overpowered the alcohol, even if only for a brief moment. Conversations such as this are exactly what I treasure about those final days. I am thankful Dad came back into my life after years of separation, and for the cherished moments we were blessed with.

After he finished the last puff of the third cigarette, I could tell his energy level wavered. He asked to go in and have some coffee. I wheeled him in, situated the wheelchair next to his bed, locked down the wheels, laid his accoutrements on the side table, and hoisted him over to the bed. I went to the kitchen and made his coffee. I put the steaming mug on his table and opened the blinds. We sat in his room sipping it together in the quiet of the early morning. That would be the last morning he would ask to go out to the garage and the last sips of coffee he would have.

Slowly throughout the next three days, the dad I knew melted away. He lost his sight, lost his hearing, and lost the ability or need to get out of bed. One eye became somewhat fixed and he didn't talk much, if at all. Restlessness increased and he pulled and tugged at his blankets and himself. I learned from the hospice nurse that this is common when the end of life nears.

We talked to him at his bedside, held his hand, and told him it was okay to leave us. In our selfishness, we didn't want him to go, but we knew his body hurt. He resisted death. He wasn't ready yet, but we didn't know what exactly he waited for. We prayed and begged God to take him so his suffering would end.

My sister Emily and I agreed to stay up to care for Dad the first night. We were tired but knew Mom could not handle sitting up all night and then taking care of him all day, too. His restlessness intensified, and he no longer found interest in watching television, smoking, or eating.

The dad I knew as a teen would give the silent treatment if I angered him somehow, if he was in a bad mood, or maybe for no apparent reason, but now he stopped talking, not out of spite or anger, but out of inability. After the long, fidgety night with Dad, Emily and I were in great need of a shower and some sleep. Mom would be the main caregiver for the day as Emily and I helped with medication. Looking back on that time, the days and nights seemed like a never-ending dream, but also oddly short. We knew Dad would not be with us long and were cherishing every moment.

Family came in and family left. When people were in the house, Dad grew intensely more restless. His family wanted to see him and show support and just simply be close to Dad, and we appreciated every last visit. People brought in food; so much food we couldn't eat it all, but it was all welcomed and appreciated. My grandma and aunt took a turn sitting with Dad. Our cousin helped Dad find comfort with essential oils and soft music. This short respite was a blessing. We knew any attempt to help Dad was born out of love and compassion for him and for us. Day two had been long, but it illustrated what Dad had always told us, "Family is important."

My daughter Leah and my husband Patrick agreed to take the first shift of the second night. They stayed awake with Dad until two in the morning, and then Emily and I planned to take the remaining time. We had gone to bed early in order to ensure we were awake and alert once our shift started. I remember being very jumpy, even in sleep. Anytime I heard a noise, or even if I didn't hear anything at all, I woke in a sudden panic. I never rested completely, much like when I came home from the hospital after giving birth to Leah—one eye opened, one eye closed, and both ears on high alert. Leah woke me so I could join Emily for our early morning vigil. Emily and I joined Patrick and Leah in the kitchen-turned-medical-center. We reviewed the last round of medications and they recounted the restless night Dad had had so far. The night had been more fitful than the previous one. His vision failed. His hearing failed. He could no longer get out of bed. He merely lay there, turning and twisting, pulling and tugging, reaching and grabbing the air. Emily and I relieved Patrick and Leah so they could rest and we sat at the kitchen table talking about the events leading up to that night.

Our first hour on duty that early morning, we paced back and forth checking on Dad, jumped when we heard a noise, chatted, and, ironically, laughed in delirious exhaustion. Even though Dad lay in the next room suffering through his last hours, Emily and I nervously found humor in our memories. That is just how we are. No disrespect for suffering, but that is how the process of grief began for us. We felt guilty at the time, but in retrospect, laughter was the best coping mechanism, especially during troubling hours.

Through our edgy fatigue, we heard Dad in his room mumbling and moaning. We went to check on him and discovered he had pulled his stomach tube out and created quite a mess. Emily went to the bathroom to throw away some of the soaked towels and I finished cleaning him up the best I could. I heard him clearly say, "He's winning." I instantly looked up and saw him reaching for the corner of the ceiling. He had a look of desperation on his face and his eyes were bulging. That moment his eyes were more alert and he spoke more clearly than he had in hours. I looked at him and (today I believe) the Holy Spirit spoke through me, "No, Dad, he is not winning. God is winning. Take his hand, Dad. Take God's hand." I stood there after I spoke these things and Dad looked directly into my eyes and said, "I can't." His own exhaustion overwhelmed him and his hand went to his forehead, rubbing it in frustration. I believed beyond my own comprehension in that moment Satan was fighting against God for Dad's soul.

Emily came back into the room and sat on the edge of the bed, while I went in search of a Bible. The Holy Spirit guided me to find my father-in-law's Bible lying on my husband's nightstand. I grabbed it and sprinted back into the living room. I opened it and searched for Psalm 23. I knew I needed to go back to Dad and begin reading this particular passage to him. I did exactly as I was led to do. I moved the stool from the corner and positioned it beside Dad's bed. I laid the open Bible on the stool and got on my knees and began reading Psalm 23 out loud, with purpose. Leading up to that moment, Dad had been extremely restless, but once I began reading, he reached for the stool. Dad stretched out his hand, groping to find the source of the words, and laid his hand on the Bible as I read aloud.

> *The LORD is my shepherd; I shall not want.*

> *He makes me to lie down in green pastures: He leads me beside the quiet waters.*

> *He restores my soul: He guides me in the paths of righteousness for His name's sake.*

> *Even though I walk through the valley of the shadow of death, I fear no evil: for You are with me; Your rod and Your staff, they comfort me.*

> *You prepare a table before me in the presence of my enemies; You have anointed my head with oil; my cup overflows.*

> *Surely goodness and lovingkindness will follow me all the days of my life: and I will dwell in the house of the LORD forever.*

I can't recall how many times I recited these words, but when I finished, Emily and I prayed to our Lord to be with Dad and guide him home. Those moments were powerful and exhausting. Overwhelmed, emotionally spent, and in shock, Emily and I left the room. Dad found rest for a few minutes, and we found comfort because we knew God was there. Through the pain, through the suffering, through the battle, God showed up.

Dad spent much of his adult life searching for something to satisfy his soul. His faith wavered and he questioned God's love for him. I innately knew after the deep prayer experience, Dad found what he had pursued for so many years. I know he hadn't realized it, but God pursued Dad over the years, too. That night God won the battle for Dad's soul.

Emily and I decided we should call the hospice nurse and chaplain. The nurse, Tammy, and chaplain, Samuel, spent five hours of their lives praying over our dad. They spent time trying to make him comfortable and peaceful to no avail. They spent time praying with us. They spent this time because they knew Dad's eternity depended upon it and for that, we are forever grateful.

Whenever I left the house during those last three days, the moment I returned, I felt the presence of God. He was there and he was in the room with Dad. Throughout the third day, Dad wanted my mother, his wife, right there by his side. If Mom left the room, Dad clearly bellowed, "Honey!" To hear him call out this familiar term of endearment after not talking directly to us in days astounded us. He did this three times that day, each time Mom would leave his side. On his deathbed, not able to hear, speak, or see, and he wanted the love of his life right there beside him. I can only describe this as love without end.

The day before he left the bed for the last time, Dad wanted a bath, a shave, and a haircut. Between my mother and my husband, he got his wish. He had his favorite soap, Irish Spring, his favorite deodorant, Lady Speed Stick, and Patrick let him use some of his cologne. When I came home from work that afternoon, Mom and Patrick told me it had been Dad's best day. I found out later that Dad told my husband, "After I am gone, I don't want them to be sad. I want them to find happiness. A house should be full of laughter." Patrick had the foresight to write that quote down and I am so glad he did.

The long day three was closing in on us. Family had been at the house most of the day and we had all the food we needed. We ate together at our table in the kitchen, just like any average day. Dad finally fell asleep long enough for Mom to get a bite to eat and rest her back from bending over his bed. The reaching, mumbling to angels, pulling, tugging, deep breathing, asking God to take him, and the frustration were slowly beginning to subside. We were all exhausted beyond measure and wondered if the end would come soon. We prepared ourselves for God to take the beloved husband, Dad, grandfather, father-in-law, son, brother, uncle, cousin, and friend—home. The time had come. It just had to.

After dinner, we each spent time with Dad. Mom was right there, at the side of his bed, holding his hand and loving him through the broken heart. We prayed over him. We each told Dad, without tears and with complete confidence, how much we loved him, how wonderful a father and grandfather he had been, and that it was time for him to stop fighting. It was time to go home and be with his Father, our loving God. We told Dad how much God loved him. We each had a turn pouring our love and our hearts out to Dad. It was the most beautiful memory I have to this day. After we were done, everyone but Mom filtered into the living room, sat together, told stories, and laughed. Mom stayed with Dad and held his hand, softly caressing it, talking him through his last breaths. Shortly after nine o'clock in the evening on Monday, August 10, 2015, Mom placed Dad's hand into God's hand. She stayed there and kissed Dad good-bye for the last time.

As quickly as Dad had reentered my life, he was gone again. In the days following his death, sorrow, regret, guilt, and confusion smothered me. Like clouds looming before a threatening storm, my world slowly grew dark. I could feel the rumbling of grief deep in my chest. I wanted to hold on to Dad just a little longer. The sober Dad. The Dad who relished laughter. The Dad who savored watermelon more than any other food on earth. The Dad who enjoyed watching the same movie over and over again until he could quote each line. The Dad whose instinct was to protect me. The Dad who loved without limits. Why had God brought Dad back to me just to take him away again so quickly? I didn't know how deeply those three weeks with him would change the course of my life and my destiny. The journey of my redemption began the night my dad found eternity with Jesus.

Chapter 1
Opening the Bottle of Blame

Submit therefore to God. Resist the devil and he will flee from you.

James 4:7

Dad's physical strength was something I marveled at. In his younger days throughout my childhood, he was a heavy equipment mechanic—the guy in a yellow hard hat you would see on the side of the road in a construction zone or at the site of the next downtown office building. It took great physical strength to work on those majestic machines.

I can still remember the smell of oil and grease when he came home from work. I remember his six-foot-three frame towering over Mom, Emily, and me. He left his Frankenstein-like, greasy steel toed work boots sitting by the garage door because my mother didn't want him traipsing through the house leaving grimy marks on her spotless floors. We rolled our eyes when his giant oil-stained hands with thick, bruised fingernails wrapped around Mom's waist as he kissed her. His majestic, Hispanic features and black wavy slicked-back hair were something people admired. They told Mom he looked like Omar Sharif and once I caught a glimpse of this regal character, I completely understood why they said it. Dad reminded me of a lion watching over his lioness and cubs—taking care of us, cooking for us, talking with us, teaching my sister and me how to take care of ourselves, protecting us, loving us.

Love is something my family does not hide. We are huggers. We speak love to each other every day when we part and every night before we go to sleep. This is normal for us. I always knew my parents were completely, utterly, inexcusably in love. They openly showed affection in front of us, leaving us without any doubts. His large hand would envelop hers in a small cage of protection. Their eyes glimmered with endless adoration when they looked at each other. Cooking together, eating together, and watching television together were things we did as a family.

Family was foremost to Dad. He came from a traditional Hispanic background, including Catholic school and strict parents. My grandparents taught him that a mother is to be honored, a father is to be respected, and family is everything. He also believed it was important for his girls to know how to take care of themselves. He knew he couldn't follow us around everywhere we went, but his instinct and focus were to protect us.

I remember being in our living room in my childhood home and my towering, deliberate dad showing me the right moves to injure my would-be attacker just severely enough to debilitate without killing him or her. He learned fighting skills in his younger days as a gang member on the streets of Dallas. He had been beaten up, stabbed more than once, and probably had brushes with the law he failed to tell me about (rightfully so). Those experiences were far in the past, and he had matured into a respectable man in society. His life on the streets taught him that although fighting is not the best answer to conflict resolution, everyone should learn some self-defense skills. Mom didn't like this idea too much, especially for Emily. She was ten years younger than me, but Dad convinced her it was important for a girl to know how to defend herself regardless of her age. He had a primal instinct to keep us safe when he was not around.

I recall being about fifteen or sixteen when Dad started drinking again after years of sobriety. He knew the steps to take to get sober and stay that way, but like a prowler lurking in the shadows, the alcohol stole his ability to abstain. I remember him leaving the house, angry at something, and driving to the liquor store. It started with beer and slowly progressed to vodka. Since vodka has virtually no odor, he thought his falling off the wagon would not be discovered. Alcoholics tend to deny what is obvious to everyone around them. They think no one will detect a change in behavior, but this is far from the truth. We could always tell. We didn't have to smell anything to know there was a difference in him.

The detection of alcohol was not just about smell, though—an even greater indication of drunkenness was his mood. He became angry and said things to us he would never say under normal circumstances. Dad was a gentle giant, but things changed when alcohol entered our lives. He left the house frequently. He stayed hidden in the bedroom with the door closed and the TV loud. He withdrew from the family. The loving familiarity dissipated.

At first, I didn't realize what was going on. I developed into a self-absorbed teenage girl with a rebellious streak. This was not normal behavior for me. Trouble began to find me. I had a mouth on me, skipped school, stole my grandmother's cigarettes and would habitually "go for a walk" to smoke.

"I'm going for a walk," I hollered to Mom, my hand on the front doorknob.

"It's freezing outside!" Mom yelled from the kitchen.

"I'll be fine!"

"Don't stay out too long. Your mother is cooking dinner." Nanny, my grandmother, sat in her recliner in the living room holding her cigarette between two perfectly manicured fingers.

"I don't think you should go, Kim. Come on, stay here and help me cook." Mom stepped through the pocket door leading from our kitchen to the living room, wiping her hands on a dish towel.

"Mom, I don't want to help you. I already have to do the dishes after dinner. Isn't that enough?" I said with my signature eye roll.

"Kim, please, I have enough to deal with. I don't need your eye rolling and arguing on top of everything."

"I said, I'll be back soon." I opened the door, unlocked the rickety screen door and let it slam behind me.

Selfishness ruled my heart like the alcohol ruled Dad's.

§

After hearing the car roar to a start and watching him back out of the driveway, Mom would come get me to help search the house for empty beer cans or liquor bottles. Their small bedroom held Dad's chair wedged closely beside their tiny closet. Inside the closet, an old hardwood hinged door in the floor led to the crawl space beneath. That would be one of the many places to search. Mom would dart from one probable hiding spot to another. We hunted for the enemy which came in a clear bottle with an all too familiar vodka brand printed in bold red letters on the front.

"Go to the crawl space and see if you can find anything." Mom stood at the front room window, peeking through the blinds. She always did this before we went on our search, just to make sure Dad had really left.

"Why do I always have to help with this?" I sulked to Mom.

"Will you just do it? Why do you have to be so argumentative?" She sounded exasperated.

My shoulders instinctively slumped and I stomped down the hallway.

"Stop stomping around!" Her voice followed me as I walked. It usually did on nights like this. We were a team of two on a scavenger hunt for evidence. It amazed me how Dad actually thought we didn't know he drank (or maybe he did), but the addiction turned out to be stronger than the conscience.

The repetitive action played like the movie *Groundhog Day* each time Dad would leave. We bent and stooped, lifted the mattress and chair cushion, me on my knees in the crawl space below the house and Mom sifting through dirty clothes in the hamper. I huffed and puffed through the hunt, convinced it was my punishment. As children of alcoholics tend to do, I blamed myself for Dad's drinking and in my young mind, Mom asking me to help confirmed my distorted thinking.

Sometimes through our searches we found two or three bottles, and other times we found nothing.

"How many did you find?" Mom and I met in the middle of their bedroom.

"I found one in the crawl space. Half full." I proudly showed off my discovery.

"Good. Take it to the bathroom and pour it out. Make sure and bury the bottle deep in the kitchen trash can."

I walked to the bathroom, unscrewed the red, metal lid of the bottle and poured its contents down the sink. The bitter smell of the vodka wafted up my nose. How could he think this stuff could not be detected? *Wishful thinking on his part*, I smirked.

"Hurry up! I think I heard the car in the driveway." Mom hurriedly switched off the bathroom light and peeked out the window to the front of the house.

"Okay, okay," I said.

It was a false alarm but she looked as if she had just seen the devil himself. Her face flushed through her pale skin.

After we accomplished our task for the night, I went to my bedroom to get some sleep. As I lay in the comfort of my bed, my mind wandered to our perpetual hunt for bottles. Why did we continue to repeat the same actions over and over again and expect different results? I secretly blamed myself for his relapse. Mom never knew this. Ironically, I kept the self-blame and shame bottled inside to prevent drawing attention to it, and left the lid screwed on tight.

What caused Dad to start drinking again? Was I to blame? I had convinced myself it was my fault. I was the cause. I vowed that night, as I did many nights, to stop my selfish behavior and control my rebellious mouth. I held myself hostage with the guilt I felt. I rehearsed in my mind over and over again how awful I was to be able to cause someone to turn to alcohol for solace. Instead of lying there wallowing in my admonishment and making empty vows to the silence of my dark bedroom, I should have sought the wisdom of the invisible being people called God. I didn't know much about him. I knew he existed but didn't realize how he could have helped comfort my aching, guilt-riddled heart.

WHERE WAS GOD?

In the early years, I imposed blame upon myself with the help of Satan's lies telling me it was my fault Dad turned back to the bottle. The enemy repeated to me I was too much to handle, so Dad had to pop the top on his first can soon after I turned fifteen.

So where was God? It is so easy for me to ask that question. I'm sure you have asked the same one countless times. I looked upon this dark place and wondered where God was. My family believed in God, however, my parents had been hurt by situations at church, and unfortunately their solution was to not attend. The scant religious exposure I received came from visiting different churches with my friends.

As a result, it did not occur to me to cry out to God. Instead, I ignored him. God never left my side, though. He was there in the darkness of my room as my heart hurt. I didn't know how to talk to him, so for years that precious practice of prayer could not reveal truth to me. Since my earthly father had turned into an unreliable person, I felt as though God must have the same tendencies. Why should I spend time investing in a relationship with God when he would eventually reject me like my own dad did? This happens so often to us as girls and later as adult women who were raised in the dysfunctional atmosphere of addiction. We tend to think of God as a person that will leave us, hurt us, or point out our faults. I know I did.

Hear me loud and clear! Those are lies that the enemy wants us to believe. Satan's deceptions become louder when we are weak. Satan prowls in the dark places, hunting for our pain (1 Peter 5:8). Satan knew my faith was weak, so his lies to my heart intensified second after second, minute after minute, hour after hour. If a voice is saying to my heart that I am not worthy of love and I am to blame for the actions of someone else, those negative words are not of God. God wants us to know how valuable we are (Matthew 10:31). His words are positive (Jeremiah 29:11).

How do we resist these evil lies? We turn to God and his word to guide our path. James 4:7 tells us, *"Submit therefore to God. Resist the devil, and he will flee from you."* Our greatest enemy is Satan and it creates a weakness in him when we resist his wiles and turn toward God. The negative words that enter our minds slowly begin to dissipate because God's word is the strongest truth there is. Period. The enemy must turn and flee because we said so, in Jesus' name. We cannot allow the sour words of the adversary to penetrate our hearts. We must stand boldly against him, resist him and his lies, and he will flee. He doesn't have a choice.

Although I didn't know how to have a relationship with my heavenly Father then, he still watched over me. Dad's love for me didn't stop because he drank too much; he simply couldn't live up to my expectations of normalcy. I did not understand why he had to drink. I had no idea that the addiction was a disease he could not control. Those feelings of self-blame are not from God, though. The feelings of rejection and hurt stem from the enemy's lies. God tells us in Deuteronomy 31:6, *"'Be strong and courageous, do not be afraid or tremble at them, for the LORD your God is the one who goes with you. He will not fail you or forsake you.'"* This promise shows me that while my earthly father had struggles with alcohol he could not control, my heavenly Father lovingly stepped in and took care of my heart.

> *Yet those who wait for the LORD will gain new strength;*
> *They will mount up with wings like eagles, They will run*
> *and not get tired, They will walk and not become weary.*

Isaiah 40:31

Chapter 2
Choosing a Path of Destruction

For God has not given us a spirit of timidity, but of power and love and discipline.

2 Timothy 1:7

When I was a young teen, Dad took a brief break from construction and began working for a family owned grocery store in town. The store had operated for generations and Mom and Nanny worked there as long as I could remember. Every employee had known me since I was small. Situated right off the main street beside a Baptist church, in a town where everyone knew everyone, the white brick building with sprawling plate glass windows and a welcoming sidewalk felt like a second home to me. When I was a young girl, Mom would drive there and let me go in by myself to buy the small list of items we needed. I walked in with my list in my hand, money in my pocket, and my head held high. I was so proud Mom trusted me to do the shopping. I'm sure she had called ahead to let my protectors who worked there know I was coming, but I didn't know at the time and didn't care.

As I grew older, the big responsibility began to feel like a burden instead of a privilege. This became truer after passing my driving test. Mom worked a lot and Dad grew less dependable to take care of things. As with many children of alcoholics, much of the adult responsibility fell on me. As a teenage girl, the highlight of going to the store was the fact I could see cute guys. That is naturally where my mind tended to wander.

I began to take notice of a brown-haired, brown-eyed guy that worked there. I looked forward to going anytime we ran out of milk, bread, or cereal. Finally, I asked Mom about him.

"So, who is that new guy?"

"What new guy?" Mom said as she stirred the spaghetti sauce in the pot on the stove.

"You know, the dark haired one at the store." I practically lay across the kitchen counter, nonchalantly twirling my frizzy hair.

"I don't know who you are talking about. We have several new people now." I saw her sneak a grin.

"You know exactly who I'm talking about. What's his name?"

"Are you talking about Patrick?" She continued to stir, avoiding eye contact.

"Well, I don't know, that's what I'm asking you!" I straightened up and put my hands on my hips.

She laughed, "If you are talking about the one that looks like Tom Cruise, Patrick is his name and he is a senior. He's too old for you so get that right out of that pretty head of yours."

I had just started my freshman year of high school. I thought to myself, *well, there goes that!*

"Oh, well, I didn't say I wanted to date him or anything. I was just curious, that's all." I played off my disappointment with a sarcastic laugh and a shrug.

I went to my room and shut the door. I had lied to Mom, of course. I did want to date that guy. I wanted to very much. There was just something about him I couldn't get out of my head. I resolved that I would talk to Dad when he came home from working in the meat market of the store. He would know more about Patrick since he worked there, too. I also knew that I could sweet-talk Dad into just about anything—before the drinking started again anyway.

If it weren't for Dad talking Mom into allowing me to go on a date, only with this special boy, at the age of fourteen, I would have never met my husband. Dad had a fondness and admiration for Patrick. He worked hard and had great respect for adults. Dad appreciated that about him. I found out many years later, he and Dad had a strong friendship then. Dad arranged for Patrick to pick me up for my first real car date.

Before he arrived, Dad reminded me of a few things. He got my attention by using a special pet name which means "little one" in Spanish.

"Mija, remember I am only allowing you to go on a date with Patrick because I trust him. I know he will take good care of you because if he doesn't, he knows what I will do to him. He's been warned already." Dad's serious expression mortified me. I couldn't believe it.

"Dad! Seriously? You threatened to kill him?"

"No, I didn't threaten to kill him. You're crazy! I did tell him I would mess him up real bad if anything happened to you."

"Dad! Oh my gosh. I can't believe you!"

"What? You are my girl. I have to protect you." He sat in his favorite chair, his legs crossed and his cigarette between two fingers.

The doorbell rang.

My heart sank to my feet—that rollercoaster downward spiral kind of feeling.

"Kim, he's here!" Mom called from the living room.

I must have looked as if I had seen an alien.

"Are you okay?" Dad chuckled.

"Yeah, just nervous. I've never been on a real date before. Especially with a senior!" My palms began to sweat.

"You'll have fun. He's a good kid. Go on now."

I willed my body to push off the edge of the bed where I sat, but it was like I had concrete in my behind.

"What are you waiting for?"

I placed my hands on either side of my hips and pushed myself up. My heart raced. I walked like a zombie to the bedroom door.

Dad cleared his throat. "Are you forgetting something?" he asked as he turned his head and pointed to his cheek.

"Oh yeah, sorry, Dad." I gave it a peck.

"Have fun. Be home by eleven," he reminded.

"Okay. I love you, Dad."

"I love you too, Mija."

"Eleven, sharp!" he called after me as I walked out of the bedroom and down the hallway. I somehow made it to the living room and Patrick stood in the front doorway, talking with Mom.

Patrick's eyes beamed when I walked in. Mom shifted her gaze to me.

"Well, it's about time," she said.

"Sorry, you know how Dad is." I laughed nervously.

I kissed Mom bye and Patrick walked me down the sidewalk to his car. I hoped he couldn't hear my heart beating as loudly as I could.

§

I fell in love with Patrick that night. I knew he was someone I could spend the rest of my life with. We dated off and on throughout my high school years. We broke up a few times, just like many teenage couples do, but we always made our way back to each other.

I felt like a queen as a freshman wearing a senior's ring and letter jacket every day to school. I know that somewhere inside I wanted the other girls to be jealous.

Dad's relapse into drinking came not long after Patrick and I began dating and intensified throughout our courtship. Like all children of alcoholics, I couldn't have a normal social life. I didn't want friends to come to my house because I didn't know if he would be drinking. Dad's normal loving nature disappeared after the bottle opened and the mood altering elixir flowed down his throat. He became angry, argumentative, and embarrassing. In contrast to my friends, I had few sleepovers, never invited friends over to study, and only rarely hosted movie nights at my house. Naturally, I stayed away as much as I could.

After Patrick graduated, he started community college. When we were not together, I worked, first at a local pizza place, then later at the "family" store. When I wasn't working, I spent time with friends. Anywhere to be away from home. When I would come home, I usually wound up arguing with Mom or Dad—yelling matches that amounted to nothing really. My rebellion intensified.

Mom never told me Dad's drinking was my fault. She never blamed me for it, but somehow, in my immature, distorted thinking, it was. I thought because I was the one that had to help Mom find the bottles, she was somehow punishing me for being the cause. I blamed myself for almost everything negative that happened in my life and in the lives of others. I found myself making a series of bad choices. I would leave school during lunch and go with friends to smoke in the alley behind some apartments across the street. I lied to my parents and skipped school to drink with friends. I began to hate myself for doing the exact things I hated in my dad. As a young girl, I was perplexed by my feelings but had no one I could turn to.

Christmas, my junior year of high school, Patrick asked me to marry him. College hadn't worked out like he thought, so he and his best friend had decided to join the Navy together. Before flying to Sinop, Turkey, and spending the next year on top of a mountain, he wanted a promise that I would wait for him. What better promise than an engagement? We agreed when he returned home on his next long leave, we would marry. I would finish high school and then join him at his next duty station. My senior year would be spent as a Navy wife.

Patrick called from Turkey, and sent gifts, while I planned a small wedding. Every red-blooded American girl's dream, right? Well, yes and no. It is difficult to be a teenage fiancé of a Navy man. Patrick was in a foreign country in the middle of the Cold War. I spent the rest of my junior year at home going to school, football games, out with my friends—all the things normal teen girls do. I didn't go to prom that year because I felt guilty having fun without him. Even though our country was not technically in wartime, it was still difficult to be separated.

I spent time with friends and Patrick served our country. I attended football games and he was monitoring the Russians. I listened to music and swooned over the eighties hair bands and he slept on a steel cot in his barracks. He was a man; I was still a girl. Thoughts of leaving my family and being in strange places with no familiar faces frightened me. I had time on my hands and began to freak out. I was too young to be a good wife, and didn't even know what it meant to be a wife. Not then. In order to be a wife, I had to know how to love, honor, and respect my husband. I didn't know how to do any of those things and certainly didn't feel worthy of love, honor, or respect from anyone. Patrick told me he loved me, but I couldn't understand why. I also had fears about getting married. I didn't want my life to turn out like my mother's.

Patrick had been in the Navy for about a year when he surprised me with a phone call saying he would arrive in Dallas later that night. My heart raced again, but this time, it was for different reasons.

"I'm not sure if I can marry you," I blurted out.

"What do you mean?" I could hear his voice quiver.

"I mean, I don't think we can get married."

Click.

He hung up the phone without another word.

I woke later that night to banging on the front door. Mom came to get me from bed.

"Kim, Patrick is here."

I didn't know what to say to him. My mind was made up. No turning back. I wasn't ready for marriage. My heart hurt anyway.

He had been drinking. I could smell it on his breath. He didn't face me at first, but when he did, his eyes were swollen. We stood on my front porch and the feelings rushed out.

"I am not ready for this," I spoke softly.

"What do you mean, you're not ready for this?" His tone was harsh and sarcastic. His words slurred.

"I mean, I just can't. I'm sorry." I didn't look at him. I couldn't.

"I don't get you. Is it somebody else?" He looked at me with contempt.

"No," I almost whispered.

"Then why?" his voice quivered again.

I didn't have an answer. He inched closer to me.

"I want—no, I need for you to look me in the eye and tell me you don't love me." He came closer.

I looked at his feet. I couldn't bring myself to lift my eyes to his.

"Kim. Look at me." He gently touched my arm, then my face.

"I can't." I fought back the tears.

"Look me in the eyes and tell me you don't love me." Tears dropped down his cheeks.

"I don't love you."

He dropped his hands from my arm and face, slowly turned and stepped off the front porch, and walked calmly to his truck parked by the curb. He opened the door, climbed in, slammed the door, turned the key in the ignition, and revved the engine. I looked away but could still hear the rocks pinging on the metal undercarriage as he sped down my street for the last time.

WHERE WAS GOD?

Have you ever felt as if you were ensnared in a tornado? Spinning across a vast landscape, picking up debris along the way and destroying everything in your path? You are not alone! At this point in my life, things were spinning out of control. Becoming an adult is difficult enough without having to deal with broken hearts and empty bottles along the way. Where was God? In order to answer that, let's first take a look at who God is:

- **Omniscient** – He knows all things – *"in whatever our heart condemns us; for God is greater than our heart and knows all things."* – **1 John 3:20**

- **Omnipotent** – He is the most powerful – *"Then Job answered the LORD and said, 'I know that You can do all things, and that no purpose of Yours can be thwarted.'"* – **Job 42:1-2**

- **Omnipresent** – He is always present – *"The eyes of the LORD are in every place, Watching the evil and the good."* – **Proverbs 15:3**

He has written our stories, he knows how they will end and is guiding us through them daily. The tricky thing here is he has also given us the gift of free will. God is kind to us and has given us the ability to choose for ourselves (Proverbs 16:9).

God created each of us in his image (Genesis 1:26). Since we have been created in the image of God, we resemble him, but do not have the ability to foresee the results of our choices. He gave us the gift of the freedom to choose any path we wish. His desire is for us to choose him.

Let's say I am walking on a safe pedestrian path parallel to a railroad track. I do not know when the train is going to come, but I move from the path beside the track and step up to walk down the middle of the track bed. As I am walking, I begin to feel the vibration of the approaching train. My sense of feeling warns my brain I should move off the track, back to the path intended for me, but I ignore the risk. I continue to walk. The train draws closer and I hear the horn blast and the sound of the wheels click-clacking against the steel track. My sense of hearing screams at my brain to move, but I ignore it and continue walking.

Eventually, the train catches up to me, causing pain and destruction. My poor choices may result in my harm as well as that of others. This is an illustration of free will and Satan's attempt to destroy our lives. We are walking a safe path away from immediate danger and then suddenly we decide to step directly in the midst of the chaos. We may feel something in our hearts trying to tell us to get back on the path, but we ignore it and keep moving. The rebellion I acted upon was exactly my choice to step on the tracks, but one God allowed. During that time in my life, every step I took, every direction I turned, I was walking down the twisting, turning railroad tracks. All the while, the train was racing up behind me blowing its horn for me to change my path, quickly.

Why did I continue to step in front of the train, resisting the safe path and taking roads that were dangerous or risky? I resisted God's best for me because I thought I wasn't worthy of love from anyone, especially from God. The enemy's lies telling me I did not deserve real love pounded in my ears. Instead of rejecting those lies and turning toward the truth of God's word, I left a path of destruction behind me as I walked away from my first love. I left shattered dreams and broken hearts along the way.

Is the train chasing you right now? Can you hear the horn blasting in your ear? Are you running down the middle of the tracks not quite knowing how to jump to safety? You are not running alone. Talk to a safe friend. Find a biblical counselor to speak with. Seek God's love to comfort you. God is right there running beside you. He will carry you if you let him. It is safe in his arms. Today is the day to stop the chaos and jump into the arms of Jesus. Say this prayer with me, won't you?

> *Heavenly Father,*
>
> *You are the all-knowing, all-powerful, all-present, loving God. Save me from the chaos that is my life right now. I trust you will take care of me and provide the right path for me to take. Today I jump into your arms. Please carry me until I can walk in the confidence of your love.*
>
> *In Jesus name, Amen.*

> *...by loving the LORD your God, by obeying His voice, and by holding fast to Him; for this is your life and the length of your days, that you may live in the land which the LORD swore to your fathers, to Abraham, Isaac, and Jacob, to give to them.*
>
> **Deuteronomy 30:20**

Chapter 3
Desperate Escape

...and My people who are called by My name humble themselves and pray and seek My face and turn from their wicked ways, then I will hear from heaven, will forgive their sin and will heal their land.

2 Chronicles 7:14

After Patrick left that night, I ran to my room and cried myself to sleep. Ending the engagement was one of the most difficult things I had done. I couldn't be the kind of wife he needed. I didn't know how to be an adult. I thought I knew what I wanted, but in my immature mind, nothing made sense. I panicked over small things, big things, things that were true and things conjured up in my mind. Instead of talking it out like an adult would, I ran from my troubles— escaping into the rooms of my mind as often as possible.

I should have immediately taken my troubles to God, but didn't realize that was an option. I should have cried out to him in desperation. I should have found a safe person to confide in. I should have asked for help and searched the Bible to learn the wonderful promises God had for me. Instead, I froze in my fear. I retreated into myself. I remained silent. I pushed people I loved away.

Anxiety consumed me then. A part of me wanted desperately to marry the man I loved, but the other part of me couldn't leave behind my familiar life, not knowing what would happen. I felt responsibility for the way Dad behaved and the way Mom reacted to it. These are the distorted thinking patterns and confusing emotions of a child of an alcoholic. There was a constant push and pull, wanting one thing, but settling for something less. I was desperate for love, but it also scared me. I wanted away from home, but couldn't leave. I wanted a normal home, but didn't know what normal meant. I flopped around like a fish out of water—wanting one thing, but doing the opposite.

I began having difficulty containing the rage within me. I was angry at myself for all of the mixed-up feelings inside. I looked for confrontation most of the time. Dad and I argued while Mom was at work. She and I argued when Dad was at work. Arguing and fighting had become our primary form of communication.

One night when Mom was at work and Dad was cooking dinner, he and I started arguing about something petty. The yelling match ended with Dad poking his stiff, strong finger into my upper chest. Yelling at me. Pushing my anger to the brink. That did it for me. I ran to my room and called the lady I worked with at an insurance agency in town.

"Shirley, can I come stay with you?"

"Well, sure you can. What's going on?"

"I can't take it here anymore. Dad's drunk again. We got into a fight," I said, almost inaudibly, tears pouring.

"Calm down now, I can barely understand you. What happened? Are you hurt?" Her motherly voice soothed me.

I sucked in a deep breath, "No, I'm not hurt physically. I just can't stay here anymore. Can you come get me?"

She agreed to pick me up. I sat on my bed shaking with rage and fear. I had no choice but to call Mom at work.

Dread washed over me. I dialed the number to the grocery store and recognized her voice immediately.

"Mom." I began to sob.

"Kim? What's wrong?"

"I've got to go. Me and Dad had a fight. I can't stay here anymore. I'm leaving." I tried not to cry.

"What are you talking about? Where are you going? Just wait. Don't do anything yet. I get off in thirty minutes. What happened?" she said frantically.

"No, Mom. I'm done." I hung up the phone before she could say anything else.

I quickly stuffed some things in a small bag. I heard Dad's heavy footsteps coming down the hall. My heart raced. I didn't want another confrontation. He didn't knock. The door swung open and banged against the wall.

"What are you doing?" Dad's usual warm, loving eyes transitioned into pools of rage.

"I'm leaving, Dad." I didn't look at him.

"And where do you think you're going?" he scoffed.

"Shirley is coming to pick me up. She is probably already here. Don't try to stop me, please." I inhaled and exhaled deep breaths. I couldn't look at him.

"I don't think so. You're only seventeen."

"Dad, please. Just let me go." I heaved my backpack over my shoulder and walked toward the doorway. Dad blocked it. I stared down at his feet.

"You are not leaving." I could smell the alcohol.

I heard a horn honk. Dad turned just enough for me to wedge between him and the door frame. I ran down the hallway toward the front door. I felt him following close behind me. I heard him stumble into the couch, but I continued out the door. I let the screen slam behind me. I ran down the sidewalk toward the Suburban.

"You can never come back if you leave now!" Dad yelled from the front porch.

I opened the car door, jumped in and slammed it shut. I didn't look back at my childhood home as she shifted the gear into drive and sped down the street.

§

I continued to go to school and work while living with Shirley. I avoided my parents, although we lived in a small town. I didn't have a car of my own so Shirley took me to school and drove me home each evening. Her two-bedroom townhome was across town from my real home. In the beginning, I was relieved to be away from the chaos. It wasn't long before loneliness set in.

The decisions I made then were based on desperation. I was desperate to do anything I could to make Dad stop drinking. Somehow I thought that if I wasn't there anymore, then surely he would stop; after all, in my mind, I was the reason he had started again. The reality was, he didn't stop drinking, and I had left Mom and Emily alone. I didn't believe he would do anything to harm them physically, he never had, but the guilt of leaving them overwhelmed me. As the dark night flooded into my room on the top floor of the townhouse, desperation, loneliness, and guilt flooded my soul. I fought against these feelings and was determined to stay away as long as possible.

This time away from home further proved to me I had made the right decision with Patrick. I missed him terribly and I still loved him, but I ached to be at home. I missed my family. Even as difficult as it was for me to live there, I still missed them. After only a few months of being away I begged to come back. They said yes without any questions. The first few days were uncomfortable and awkward, but before long, we settled back into routine. I buried the episode with Dad deep in my soul and didn't speak of it again. We just pretended everything was fine, a skill we had mastered well.

During my short stint as a runaway, I began dating a boy in my class. We only dated for a few months and went to senior prom together. Rumor had it he was seeing another girl behind my back. I confronted him about the accusations, but he denied them. It was high school drama at its best.

My anger continuously boiled under the surface. One evening, suspended between self-control and fury, I called a friend and she agreed to take me to look for the cheating boy. We drove around the suburbs of Dallas until we found him. I could hardly believe my eyes when I saw his red Ford Bronco sitting at a red light. I could see a girl sitting beside him in the passenger seat.

"There he is!" I yelled at my friend.

"I see him."

"Pull up there beside him!" The fury bled through my voice.

I completely blacked out with wrath. My friend told me later what had happened. As we pulled up beside his vehicle, I took a tire iron out from under the seat of her car. Before her car had completely stopped, I got out in the middle of traffic and ran up to the passenger side where the other girl sat. Yelling obscenities, I reared back like a batter in the bottom of the ninth inning and swung the tire iron at the window. Shards of glass flew into the vehicle and showered her as she tucked into a ball to shield herself. As the light turned green, I grabbed hold of the gaping hole and prepared to climb into the truck. I lost my grip as he burned off.

In an instant, I awoke from the rage-filled blackness. I looked down at my bleeding hands, stunned, and carried the heavy iron back to my friend's car. Angry tears flowed from my eyes. I know my friend must have thought I had completely lost my mind, and perhaps for a few moments I had. My three best friends—anger, desperation, and distorted thinking—devoured my mind that night. Filled with contempt for the way my life had turned out, I couldn't see past that moment. She didn't say a word as I opened the passenger door and dejectedly climbed in. She drove me back home to face my parents. At their insistence, I called my boyfriend's mother and confessed what I had done. She seemed sympathetic and graciously accepted my apology.

The next day, I went to work at the grocery store as I did every weekend. The boy I dated worked there, too. I decided to end the relationship and apologize for destroying his property. He arrived to work an hour later than I did, but before I had an opportunity to speak with him, I saw two uniformed officers come through the glass doors. I stood in the checkout area and watched them walk to the office. My heart raced. Surely they were not there to see me.

I quickly turned away and tried to ignore them. Then the owner called me to his office. I opened the door, walked up the stairs, and faced him and the other men.

"Yes, I'll see if they'll wait until you get here but I can't make any promises," he said as he held the phone receiver to his ear. "Okay, I'll do what I can." He hung up the phone and looked at me.

"Kim, these men are here to talk to you. Do you know why?"

I looked at them and said, "Yes, I believe I do." I could hear the thumping of my heart in my ears.

"I'm going to step out. Your mom and dad are on their way up here." He rose from his desk and placed his hand on my shoulder as he walked out.

The officers arrested me and took me to the sheriff's office. Thankfully, Dad knew the sheriff and I didn't have to actually go into a cell. They booked me in and out quickly. I was released to Dad waiting in the lobby. I learned the hard way anger and desperation cost not only a lot of money, but also cost respect for myself. My life had truly spun out of control.

On the heels of this insanity, another boy I worked with at the grocery store told me how he would treat me better. He told me he was the answer to my troubles and he would do anything for me. Those promises grabbed my attention. That is exactly what I lacked in my life. I needed someone who would treat me well and make me forget the feelings that gripped me after the night I rejected Patrick. I wanted him back, but I thought he would never want me back after I hurt him like I did. I settled for the empty promises of another.

WHERE WAS GOD?

Oftentimes, we feel as if we are completely alone. We are so desperate for normalcy, love, affection, affirmation, and acceptance we are willing to go to great lengths to find what we crave. Blinded by desperation, it's difficult to see God in the frequent heartaches, disappointments, and empty promises of the world. Many adult women of addicted parents struggle to believe that God's promises are constant and true. God doesn't lie, he can only speak truth.

We find his truth by searching his word.

- He promises rest in Matthew 11:28-29: *"'Come to Me, all who are weary and heavy-laden, and I will give you rest. Take My yoke upon you and learn from Me, for I am gentle and humble in heart, and YOU WILL FIND REST FOR YOUR SOULS.'"*
- He promises strength in Isaiah 40:29: *"He gives strength to the weary, And to him who lacks might He increases power."*
- He promises he will supply our needs in Philippians 4:19: *"And my God will supply all your needs according to His riches in glory in Christ Jesus."*
- He promises peace in John 14:27: *"'Peace I leave with you; My peace I give to you; not as the world gives do I give to you. Do not let your heart be troubled, nor let it be fearful.'"*

Satan's primary goal is to slither his way into our minds and our hearts. He desires for us to be strangled by his lies.

- Satan lies to us and says, "You can't fight against me because I know how to wear you down." **God's Word tells us our God is a powerful God. We must** *"...be* *strong in the Lord and in the strength of His might. Put on the full armor of God, so that you will be able to stand firm against the schemes of the devil."* – Ephesians 6:10-11

- Satan lies to us and says, "You are weak and have no defense against me." **God's Word tells us we have hope in God Almighty and we must** *"Be strong and let your heart take courage, All you who hope in the LORD."* – Psalm 31:24
- Satan lies to us and says, "You should be angry and seek revenge for what people have done to you." **God's Word tells us**, *"A fool always loses his temper, But a wise man holds it back."* – Proverbs 29:11
- Satan lies to us and says, "You don't need God to provide anything, I will show you how to do it yourself." **God's Word tells us,** *"And my God will supply all your needs according to His riches in glory in Christ Jesus."* – Philippians 4:19
- Satan lies to us and says, "You don't need peace, you should show everyone your fury!" **God's Word tells us**, *"And the seed whose fruit is righteousness is sown in peace by those who make peace."* – James 3:18

If we listen to these lies we will not see how God walks with us through our troubles. That is precisely what Satan wants. He doesn't want us to realize Jesus is the rest when we are weary. Jesus is the strength when we are weak. Jesus fills the needs of our hearts. Jesus is the peace in the midst of our unrest. Satan wants to keep us in the state of desperation. Jesus wants our freedom to fall into his grace. Although we may choose to seek answers from the world and from worldly things, Jesus will never leave our side. All we have to do is seek him first and he will do the rest. Take a stand against Satan by filling your mind with Scripture and shut the enemy up.

I felt tired, weak, needy and in chaos, not because God wasn't there, but because Satan had a firm grip on me. I believed the lies the enemy whispered to my heart. I didn't know any better, really. God knew that, too. Remember, he is the omniscient God. He knows all things about all of his children.

Do you feel in a state of insanity today? Has life become unmanageable for you? Pick up your Bible and seek his promises. God is our Father, our creator, and he loves each of us as his children.

- We are his children – *"But as many as received Him, to them He gave the right to become children of God, even to those who believe in His name."* – **John 1:12**
- He loves us so much he sent his only son to die for our sins – *"But God demonstrates His own love toward us, in that while we were yet sinners, Christ died for us."* – **Romans 5:8**
- He wants us to live a peaceful life free from desperation – *"'For I know the plans I have for you,' declares the LORD, 'plans for welfare and not for calamity to give you a future and a hope.'"* – **Jeremiah 29:11**

He desperately wants you to know how much he loves you. The book of John paints the vivid picture of God's love for us. Start there. Let God show his love for you through his Word.

"If I should say, 'My foot has slipped,' Your lovingkindness, O LORD, will hold me up."

Psalm 94:18

Chapter 4
Unworthy of Love

Be of sober spirit, be on the alert. Your adversary, the devil, prowls around like a roaring lion, seeking someone to devour.

1 Peter 5:8

I dated the boy who had made bold promises for about six months when I discovered I was pregnant. We married in a simple ceremony at a small church. I wore black slacks and a black maternity top—little did I know at the time how wearing black to my wedding would be so appropriate. We repeated our vows in front of the preacher and the couple who cleaned the church each week. I pushed the drifting thoughts of Patrick and my dreams of having a beautiful wedding out of my mind. The ceremony lasted about fifteen minutes. Then we drove to a hotel in the neighboring town across the highway from a popular country dancehall. We picked up tacos and headed to our room.

On the way up, we ran into some people he knew.

"Hey! Why don't ya'll come with us? We're going across the street," one of them said.

"That's sounds good! Let us go eat and we'll join you," my new husband told them.

We walked down the dingy hallway and found our room. He stuck the key in the door, turned the knob and we went in.

"I was kind of hoping to stay in. It is our honeymoon after all," I said without hiding my disappointment.

"No, I want to go. You stay here if you want."

He ate his tacos quickly, downed the drink, grabbed his keys and left. The door slammed shut behind him. I sat on the bed, alone with my thoughts.

I realized in those moments I had made a critical mistake. As I sat in the hotel room on what should have been one of the most joyful nights of my life, my mind traveled back to Patrick. Why had I let him go? Why had I lied to him on my front porch that night? How could I have told him I didn't love him, when I truly did? As I labored over these questions, I felt more unloved than ever. I wanted a normal life. I wanted a happy marriage and children. I wanted a family filled with laughter. I wanted a husband who didn't need alcohol to enjoy being around me. I just didn't know how to find it.

That night was the beginning of years of misery for me. During our eleven years together, we had two beautiful children. Leah, our firstborn baby girl, with her strawberry blonde Shirley Temple ringlets and squinty-eyed smile, was the first human I could love who would love me back unconditionally. When our son came along eighteen months after Leah was born, my little family seemed complete. I felt truly loved when my kids and I were together, but those were the only moments of happiness in my first marriage.

One desperate afternoon—after a huge fight with my husband—I decided life had become entirely too much for me to handle and everyone would be better off without me. My heart ached as I sat on the bathroom floor contemplating the best way to escape my pathetic life. Taking pills seemed the easiest and least painful method. I opened the medicine cabinet and reached for the bottle of pain pills left over from some dental work. I felt a sudden twinge deep in my heart—which I know today to be the Holy Spirit—telling me to call someone for help. I called a suicide hotline and they helped me realize suicide was not the way.

After that phone call, I was compelled to open the Bible Mom had given me for Christmas a few years prior. I turned to the first chapter, like I would with any other book. In the case of the Bible, I learned later, that is not necessarily the place one should begin reading. I fumbled my way through Genesis, but became frustrated due to a lack of understanding. I closed the book and laid it on my nightstand.

I looked at it before falling asleep each night. It caught my eye as I dressed in the mornings. I thought about it as I waited for the bus with the kids. My heart ached for love and I felt love when I held that book. Loneliness smothered me. Sadness gripped me. I needed to find somewhere to go to get away, even if it was just for a little while. I needed to be somewhere I could feel worthy again. I couldn't understand why the inner urging to read the Bible continued to grip me. I had heard somewhere—although I couldn't remember where—how Jesus loved me, but I knew that could not possibly be true. My own husband had reminded me regularly over the years how unlovable I was. He convinced me that my parents only loved me if we gave them money or if they could use me to help run their errands for them. These periodic barbs pierced my mind and confused me.

I didn't have a car of my own for several years. One morning, I walked to the local convenience store to buy cigarettes and a newspaper. I turned each page as I sat at the small dining table, listening to Barney singing *"I love you, you love me"* in the living room while the kids ate Cheerios and drank from sippy cups. While nursing my coffee I scanned the obituaries, weekly crime report, want ads, and small town news stories—the same boring gossip from the week before, just different names and faces. The church registry page caught my eye that morning.

I scanned the page as I had done every Thursday morning since the kids were born. One ad seemed to jump at me: *"Looking for love? Come visit us and you will find it. God is love!"*

I sat the cup on the table and slowly walked to the sink to start the dishes. I stared out the kitchen window and thought about the ad. I knew the church. I passed by it sometimes when I took the kids for walks around the neighborhood. I knew it was a Baptist church. I knew it was small. That was all I knew. My eyes fixed on the oak tree standing tall outside the kitchen window. The limbs swayed in the wind as a storm began to close in. The clouds bellowed across the blue blanket of sky. Tears formed in my eyes as I turned to look at the kids sitting in front of the television, Barney still teaching them about love. I closed my eyes and whispered, *"Can someone love me?"*

That instant, my heart surged and began thumping in my ears. I couldn't explain it, but I immediately sensed the need to visit the church down the street. Simultaneously, I had an overwhelming fear. I had not grown up in church. I didn't know what to expect. Thoughts cluttered my mind like the sink full of dirty dishes before me. Fear that my husband would forbid me from going, like he did so many other things, enveloped my heart. I swiped the thought to find a church from my mind, and started the dishwater.

Each week I read the paper and each week, that page screamed at me. A few months passed before I found the courage to find a church listed on the page and go. I fought against the doubts that entered my mind, particularly those that told me my husband wouldn't allow it. I examined the page one afternoon while I waited for the school bus to arrive. My eyes were drawn to the same church with the ad about God's love. I decided that would be the one.

The kids and I dressed on the following Sunday. My husband had left early the previous morning, so I wasn't concerned about having to explain where we were going. Knowing his pattern, he would not arrive home again until late Sunday night. My palms sweaty and my heart pounding, I held the kids' hands and we entered the building. Almost immediately, I felt peace. The kind of peace you feel when you are young and come home from school and your mom is there waiting for you. You know you are home.

We were welcomed with smiles and friendly people. I simply knew it was where I needed to be—a place I could flee to for a short time each week. Surprisingly, my husband did not say a word about it and I was grateful for that. I did speculate about his lack of disdain. Maybe because it was church, he chose not to complain. Maybe he didn't care anymore.

My kids quickly started looking forward to going. I enrolled them in a youth program that met every Wednesday night and while they were there, I joined in Bible study. I wanted to learn everything I could as quickly as I could. I took my Bible with me everywhere and read it during every free moment. I took notes and tried memorizing Scripture even though I struggled to understand much of it. As I read, studied, and prayed, a common theme slowly began to emerge—LOVE.

The church experience had a newness to it that I enjoyed. I had visited churches in the past either on my own or with friends, but never found a place I belonged. I didn't know what my beliefs truly were and didn't know how to find out. I was a lost girl wandering around searching for something that I couldn't quite identify. I had no purpose. Going to church in my late twenties seemed different.

I slowly learned God loved me no matter what I had done in the past. I found this difficult to understand at first, but wanted to know more. I learned how being saved meant I would live eternally in heaven with God. I watched each week as different people would walk up to the altar, kneel, pray, and cry. I wondered what they were doing. I watched as the pastor would kneel beside them, his hand resting gently on their shoulders. Sometimes he cried with them. I learned later this was an invitation to pray for healing, help, or ask Jesus to save them. The terms salvation, born again, and eternity were foreign to me. I started asking questions during my Bible studies on Wednesdays and Sunday mornings.

With the help of the men and women in my studies, I learned of God's desire to spend eternity with his people. I learned how much he loves us all, and how he sent Jesus to die on the cross for us. I finally figured out God actually does love me.

One Sunday morning during the invitation, I felt drawn to go up to the front of the church and ask the preacher how to pray for salvation.

"I'm not sure how to do this," my voice shook.

"There's not a rulebook," he smiled softly as he placed his hand on my shoulder. "Just kneel, close your eyes, and say what you feel."

I knelt at the front of the sanctuary, my hands shaking as I clasped them together. The tears dripped on the maroon carpet beneath me.

"God, I hope you can hear me. I'm in trouble. I need your help. I don't know what to do anymore. I don't know who I am. Do you know?"

The pastor had knelt beside me and had a hand on my shoulder. Emotion washed over me and I felt a huge release.

"Do you want to ask Jesus to be your personal savior?" he asked.

I nodded my head as tears continued to flow.

I continued to ask for forgiveness and prayed for salvation. For the first time since I was a child, I felt a peace that I could not explain. I was flooded with true joy. I looked forward to going each week and being around people that were like me—people who knew what it meant to be loved. I was baptized one Sunday morning, with my children sitting in the pews watching. As the pastor asked me if I had invited Jesus into my heart to be the Lord of my life, he leaned my body backward and dunked me in the warm water. As I rose from the water, my hair dripping on my shoulders, my children and the entire congregation celebrated by clapping. I finally understood what being "born again" really meant.

I started to feel as though my life had meaning again. I realized staying home all day only fueled my depression. My children, now ages seven and nine, were both in school and had grown out of naps and Barney songs. The natural next step for me was to find a job. I had sporadic jobs over the years, but had not been allowed to keep them long. My husband told me I needed to be home to raise the children

Armed with a newfound faith and confidence, I took a job at a local bank as a teller. Working in a bank awarded me great relationships with the regular customers and friendships I will never forget. I slowly realized through conversations with friends I made at work how their husbands and their lives seemed to have what mine lacked. I realized mine was not normal. Husbands are supposed to show love to their wives. Husbands are supposed to spend time with their family. Husbands are not supposed to be angry and leave their wives alone.

I learned the same thing going to church and Bible study each week. I felt the presence of God more than I ever had in the past. I learned I had choices, could make my own decisions, and was a person apart from my husband. I was worthy of love and loved by God. Once I had him in my life, things started moving in a whole new direction.

§

After twelve years and too many fights to count, my first marriage was over and instead of turning back to God when I needed him the most, I chose to turn toward dating again. I felt as if I had disappointed God. From what I learned in church, God hated divorce so I felt as though he would not be able to love me again after doing something he hates so much. Loneliness gripped me again. I needed to feel worthy of love.

I met my second husband before my first divorce had become final. We married almost one year later. He had custody of his two beautiful children. The seven-year-old and five-year-old both had dark brown eyes and brown hair. They seemed starved for love from a motherly figure. I was starved for love from anyone who would give it to me. My children, especially Leah, didn't like the idea of having to share me with his children. The kids fought a lot, but I was determined to have a normal family. At that stage in my life, normal was something I had searched for, but couldn't quite find.

Our marriage started out draped in a veil of contentment, but before long we were both drinking a lot. We sent the kids to their grandparent's house and invited people over for parties which lasted into the early morning hours. Getting drunk on the weekends became the new normal. I found when I drank, I forgot about the pain I brought with me into the marriage. The day after, though, I was filled with a different kind of pain—I was turning into my dad, something I swore I would never do.

Church had become a distant memory. I focused on my new life. I tried everything to be the perfect wife, perfect mother, and have the perfect home. We lived modestly and that was okay with me, at least I had the freedom to have friends and go places if I wanted to. I enjoyed spending time with the kids and helping with their school projects. I was able to chaperone field trips without feeling the need to explain myself to anyone. My first husband questioned almost every move I made, but my second husband didn't ask me about anything.

About a year into my marriage, Leah had difficulty going to school. During one year she had many changes in her life and at the delicate age of thirteen, it was almost too much for her to bear. Her parents had divorced, puberty struck, a new family had been introduced, she gained new siblings, moved to a new city—twice—and had started a new school. I was selfish to think she would be fine with so many changes going on. She wasn't fine.

I decided to quit work and homeschool her for at least a year. That year was one of the best years we had together. I ran a very tight ship with her education at home. We studied Shakespeare, I taught her about balancing a checkbook, having a job, paying bills, and of course the usual reading, writing, and arithmetic. She actually enjoyed our class days most of the time. I had a curriculum and a schedule that we stuck to, including lunch.

This commitment took a toll on time with the other children. At certain points, I felt like I was not being fair to everyone. Being a stepparent proved to be challenging, especially in the beginning. I often felt inadequate. I couldn't spread my attention between two younger children who needed a mother so desperately and a daughter who struggled with high anxiety and depression. The children began fighting about small things and I couldn't control them. The youngest boy's grades suffered and I couldn't figure out how to help him. Inner doubt crept in and threatened me. Depression was a companion that stuck around for the years that followed. I slowly discovered how unhappy I had become with myself. Discontentedness snuck up on us within five years of our marriage. One can only fake normal and happiness for so long.

§

During my second marriage, Nanny was diagnosed with Alzheimer's disease. Not long after her diagnosis, she went to live with Mom and Dad. While caring for her ailing mother, Mom also struggled with Dad's frequent job losses, their lack of money, and the gripping albatross of addiction. Piles of medical bills mounted on her roll top desk, the cover pulled closed to hide them from everyone, including herself.

As Nanny's illness worsened and hospice nurses became a permanent fixture in the tiny duplex apartment where my parents lived, Dad informed Mom he planned to move out as soon as Nanny died. This announcement surprised and confused me. My anger toward him grew and the resentment deepened. I found it difficult to visit very often. This was due not only to distance—I had moved over eighty miles away soon after my second marriage—but because I found it too painful to watch the Nanny I knew slowly fade away from our family. Of course, there was also my silent contempt for what Dad had become.

Nanny left this world to be with God in heaven in late October. Dad left Mom the following February. The day after he left, I drove to my old hometown and picked Mom and her things up. An uneasy silence accompanied us on the trip to my home.

My second husband had not been happy about the decision, but I had given him no choice. Mom would come to live with us regardless how he felt about it. His drinking had become more frequent, but so had mine. Almost every weekend we had parties.

The honeymoon seemed over. He drank, I drank, and depression seeped into both of us. We lived in the same house, but that summed up our marriage. We became more like roommates than husband and wife.

One summer night, we decided to get out of the house—we stopped just short of calling it a date. Mom stayed with the kids and we went to a local bar to shoot some pool. I hadn't been anywhere since Nanny died and Mom moved in. We wound up at a bar in a town close by. I had vowed I wasn't going to drink anything because I knew that my husband would be drinking. After all, I was the responsible one. I was the one who took care of everything. It was only logical I be the designated driver. I knew how drinking and driving could destroy lives. Dad had a few DUIs and how lucky he had been to not have killed anyone or himself.

The bar we went to was a dive with a full bar situated directly across from the front entrance. I noticed the haggard older lady behind the counter sucking on a cigarette, laughing and talking with a heavier set man sitting on an old stool. He sipped on a glass of caramel colored liquid. The place was small but had enough room for one pool table tucked in the back corner and a small dance floor in the middle. I looked across the dark, smoky room and thought, *I don't know about this place.* We found a seat at the bar and husband number two asked for a beer for him and for me.

"No thanks, I'm good."

"Come on! Just one. We are here to get away and relax for a little bit."

"Okay, but just one."

One turned into two and two turned into three. Three turned into I can't recall how many I had that night. It was as if Satan was watching and delighting in the events that unfolded. My husband was playing pool in the corner with someone we didn't know. I could hear the guttural laughter as I sat at the bar sipping on my beer. His obnoxious phase set in. Even though country music played loudly through the haze of alcohol, his guffaws permeated my ears.

"How about a Vegas Bomb?" the bartender asked me in a gravelly voice.

"I don't know what that is," I slurred.

"It's a Red Bull and vodka." She leaned in closer and I could smell the liquor on her breath.

I had not been a fan of vodka. It reminded me too much of late night scavenger hunts for Dad's stash.

"I don't know, I better not. I'm driving home tonight." I nodded my head toward my husband.

"Oh, he'll be over there playing for another hour or two. Come on, you'll love it."

Without a response from me, she grabbed a short glass and set it on the bar top. As she cracked open the energy drink, she grabbed a tall bottle of clear liquid from beside her. She poured both into the glass simultaneously and slid the glass to me.

I stared at it, thinking how bad of an idea the "night out" was turning out to be. If only I had more self-control, more of an awareness of the patterns I repeated. Patterns I despised so much growing up under the shadow of my dad's selfish addiction.

I picked up the glass and took a sip. Turned out I liked the dangerous concoction. I don't know how many of those bombs I had downed when I heard a ruckus going on from the pool table corner. I whipped my head around and saw my husband and the stranger having serious words. They stood toe-to-toe and shouted in each other's faces. I immediately stumbled up from the barstool and urged him to leave.

"Come on, let's go," I slurred.

"I'm not ready to go just yet!" he yelled.

"I am, I'm not feeling well," I lied, hoping it would prevent a fight from breaking out.

He attempted to look at me, but he could barely stand straight without bobbling back and forth. Finally, he staggered over to the door.

The bartender shouted at us before we made it all the way out the door telling us to take a different route home in order to avoid the inevitable cops that would be in waiting on the main highway. I was completely lost and had no idea how to get home, not to mention neither of us had any business operating a vehicle.

I loaded him in the truck and staggered to the driver's side. I wasn't thinking clearly, but I knew he couldn't drive. I felt as if I could do a better job than him, like usual. The alcohol induced sickness was about to set in and we would have some major issues if I didn't get us home.

I stuck the key into the ignition and turned the engine over. I wasn't used to driving his truck, but was determined to sober up and pay very close attention to my surroundings. He tried to tell me where to go per the instructions he could remember from the bartender. We wound up driving down a dark country rock road. I came to a stop where dirt met pavement. The trees were large and hung heavily over the road. I couldn't see if anything was coming or not, so I inched forward until I could see to my left. I didn't see any cars coming and I pulled out onto the road. I realized that I was on the highway access road and I knew where I was. That was a good thing because I heard snoring from the passenger seat.

I turned on my blinker and was about to enter the highway when I saw the red and blue lights flashing mockingly in my rearview mirror.

WHERE WAS GOD?

As I watched the police car in my review mirror that night, flashes of Dad appeared in my mind. Had I turned into an alcoholic? What had I done? Why had I gotten behind the wheel and made the choice to drive? I looked down at the steering wheel after I pulled over to the side of the dark highway access road. I glanced up at the mirror again and saw the fear in my eyes.

I had lost all feeling of self-worth and dignity. God did not feel remotely close to me from the time I divorced my first husband up to that point, but who was to blame? God? Certainly not. God doesn't move away from us, we move away from him. Even though I became a Christian in my late twenties, my life had become a page from the parable of the farmer sowing his seeds.

In the parable, Jesus describes to his disciples a farmer planting his seeds. His teaching tells of the different ways a seed is sown and the results of each. One farmer's seeds fell on the path, the birds swooped in and ate them; some of his seeds fell among the rocks with little dirt, although the seeds sprouted quickly, the sun burned them up because there were no roots; more seeds fell among the thorns and were choked out by the weeds; other seeds fell among the good soil and they grew roots and produced a flourishing crop (Matthew 13:1-8).

I relate closely to the seed that fell in the thorns. *"'Others fell among the thorns, and the thorns came up and choked them out'"* (Matthew 13:7).

In the beginning of my walk with Christ, I felt strong and unstoppable, however, I quickly allowed the thorns around me to choke out my faith in Jesus. These thorns came in many forms:

- **struggle** with Dad's addictions,
- **anger** and **resentment** caused by Dad's choices,
- **pain** from my first marriage,
- **grief** over the loss of Nanny,
- **guilt** from not being more supportive of Mom during her pain,
- **regret** from breaking off my engagement to Patrick, and
- **unhappiness** with my second marriage.

These thorns choked out the tender plants of love Jesus had sown in my heart. I stopped caring about having a virtuous life or what God thought of me. I felt unlovable because it seemed as if every man in my life started loving me, but eventually stopped anyway. Many adult children of alcoholics believe this erroneous thought pattern. We feel unworthy of love as a result. Why should God be any different? Since I have done wrong, why would God continue to love someone like me?

That is not God's nature. It is as simple as that. God's love does not fail us. Period. This promise is repeated throughout the Bible, but one stands out the most.

> *"But you, O Lord, are a God merciful and gracious, slow to anger and abounding in steadfast love and faithfulness." –*
> *Psalm 86:15 (ESV)*

Read it again. His love for us is steadfast, abounding, faithful, merciful, and gracious. Did you see that? Let's dive in, swim around, and soak up each of those words.

- **Steadfast** – Firm and unwavering in purpose, loyalty, or resolve
- **Abounding** – To be present in large numbers or quantities
- **Faithful** – Consistently trustworthy and loyal, especially to a person, promise or duty
- **Merciful** – Showing mercy or compassion to somebody
- **Gracious** – Full of tact, kindness and politeness

(all references from the Encarta Dictionary)

As we soak in these promises, remember this—regardless of the feelings we may have of not being worthy of love, there is hope for redemption. Our God is firm, consistent, trustworthy, loyal, compassionate, and kind. We are created by him to be loved by him. Our past does not define our future—rather our future is established by God. Our sin has been washed away by the blood of Jesus Christ.

> *"But God demonstrates His own love toward us, in that while we were yet sinners, Christ died for us."*

> **Romans 5:8**

Chapter 5
Prisoner of Shame

for all have sinned and fall short of the glory of God.

Romans 3:23

My heart fell to the pit of my stomach. I couldn't comprehend what was happening to me. Every moment felt like a horrible dream. If I could somehow wake up, it would all be over and I would be fine. I screamed for the sleeping passenger to wake up. He was groggy at first, until I shouted in his ear that the cops had stopped us. His eyes bulged with comprehension and his drunken stupor faded quickly. He told me just to play it cool and everything would be fine.

The officer knocked on my window.

"Ma'am, I need for you to step out of the vehicle." I rolled down the glass.

"What did I do, sir?" I asked.

"Have you been drinking tonight?"

"Just a few," I said, as if he hadn't heard that lie a million times before.

"Go ahead and step out of the vehicle."

I did as he asked. I wore sandals and stood on the dark unlevel road. He instructed me to perform various tasks from standing on one foot to hopping up and down. I brought my finger to my nose repeatedly and attempted to recite the alphabet backwards—a feat I still find challenging being completely sober and of sound mind.

"Ma'am, I'm going to ask you to turn around and place your hands behind your head. You are under arrest for driving while under the influence of alcohol. You have the right to remain silent . . ."

The scene around me muted as the crushing fist of reality hit me in my gut. My husband and the officer spoke in muffled tones. Through my tears, everything occurred in slow motion. The officer told me to turn around and face the car. He placed handcuffs on my wrists and I felt the pinch of the cold metal against my skin. He escorted me to the patrol car, opened the door and gently guided me into the backseat. I hung my head in disgrace and shame.

As we drove for what seemed like hours, I apologized repeatedly to the officer, as if I had done something to him personally.

The officer pulled into the brightly lit secured entry of the county jail. I sobbed pathetically and couldn't bring myself to raise my head. The darkness of the night seemed to have hidden me from my bad choices, but I knew once I entered the brightly lit jail lobby, my shame would be exposed. I squinted through my puffy sockets and tried to see where I was. The officer opened the back door of the squad car and helped me to my feet.

He walked with his hands on mine behind my back and led me through the steel door of the jail. The slamming metal startled me. I heard people talking, but the fog of alcohol and misery kept comprehension at bay. He continued to lead me into a room with a female officer and released the handcuffs.

"Have a seat, please," the woman said without looking up. She continued to write on a piece of paper.

I did as I was told and sat in the metal chair.

"I need to conduct a Breathalyzer now."

She gathered her supplies and instructed me to blow several times into the machine. Never saying a word, she read the output screen and made notes.

Once the test was completed, she walked me to the front desk. I looked around and saw the cold, gray walls of the massive room. A towering circular counter sat prominently in the middle and floor-to-ceiling metal doors lined the wall behind it. Cells, like the ones on television. But this wasn't television. This was real. I felt like a twelve-year-old child amid a room of strange uniformed people. It felt as if their condemning eyes were boring holes in me, and my shame grew deeper.

The female in uniform led me over to an area with a camera and took my mug shot. The flashes of humiliation stung my eyes. The night's events tumbled in my mind. How had I been dumb enough to think I could drive after drinking what I had? My heart ached with disgrace.

Once the formalities were over, she took me to an empty cell. I looked into the small room with its cold, silver toilet and dull metal cot hanging from the wall and broke down in tears again. I shuffled in and the bars clanked behind me. I sat on the metal cot and buried my face in my hands.

I had no idea what time it was, but I knew Mom would worry if she hadn't heard from me. I asked the officer on duty if I could use the phone to call home.

"In a little while," he said coldly.

"I just need to call my mother. She has my kids."

He ignored me and continued to write something on a piece of paper in front of him. Maybe he just pretended to write something so he wouldn't feel the need to respond. I was so sorry for what I had done, but he didn't care. I was no different to him than any of the other criminals that streamed through there every day.

It seemed as though hours had passed and I gathered the courage to ask again.

"Can I please call home and talk to my mother?"

Silence.

"I know I get one phone call. When does that happen?"

Nothing.

I dropped my face and the tears flowed again.

"Please just let me check on my kids," I heaved between sobs.

"If they are with your mother, they are fine," he said without looking up.

"But when do I get my one phone call?"

Silence again.

I conceded and went back to the metal cot. I hadn't slept in hours and the night's events were exhausting, but I was fearful of sleep. I couldn't find peace through the echoing noises. I felt like I was being watched even though when I looked around, nobody glanced my direction. I felt so incredibly guilty for driving while intoxicated. The guilt hovered over me like a dark cloud.

My mind wandered to my children. I hoped my husband had arrived home somehow and Mom knew what was going on. I hoped they were getting off to school and she covered up for me. Ashamed of my choices, I couldn't fathom the thought of them knowing their mother was in jail.

A woman with a food cart rolled up in front of my cell and pushed a tray onto the floor. The blue tray held a cheese sandwich and a carton of milk. I picked up the milk and although warm, I drank it. I left the empty carton and the sandwich on the tray and went back to my cot to lie down. As I closed my eyes, a spirit of despair and abandonment seemed to suck the oxygen from the cell. I finally decided to pray. I begged God, silently.

"God, if you are still there, can you please get me out of here? I'm so sorry for what I have done. I need to be home with my kids. I can't take it here anymore. Please help me," I whispered into my tear-filled hands.

Four hours passed before my husband posted my bail.

Fatigue overcame my emotions and I sat in the same truck I drove the night before and rode home. I wanted to lie down in my own bed and get some sleep. I wanted to be left completely alone.

"I called work for you," my husband said.

"What did you tell them?" My heart raced and my eyes bulged as I turned my face toward him.

"I just told them that you had a bug or something."

"Thank God."

"What did you think I would tell them?"

"I didn't know. I just hoped you wouldn't tell them the truth. I can't lose that job."

"I think I know that." I heard disappointment in his voice, but I didn't care. I didn't think he was capable of taking care of anything important. I was the one who always took control of situations. I managed our finances, our children, and our home.

I blamed my circumstances on my husband. I shouldn't have, but I did. If he hadn't had the idea to go to the bar, I would not be facing a DUI charge. If I had never met him, I wouldn't have had to be on probation for three years. If I had not married him, I wouldn't have had to keep my secret of being a criminal from everyone. Shame and bitterness settled in and found a home in my soul after the horrible choices I made that night. Of course, these feelings were misplaced. I had made the choices myself. I shouldn't have blamed him or anyone else; what I had done was a shameful act. The thought of a tragedy occurring as a result still haunts me today.

I kept my feelings bottled inside during those years. I deflected the self-blame onto others. Even after my arrest and conviction, I couldn't trust God or anyone else. I was self-absorbed, full of resentment, and not in love with the person I was married to anymore. When I looked in the mirror, I didn't even recognize myself. I withdrew into my writing—into my own mind. I wanted to be left alone and didn't want to talk to anyone. This spiral of depression and withdrawal took control of my life, soul, and mind.

After being married to my second husband for almost seven years, I decided I didn't want to be his wife anymore. I couldn't take the way I lived. I put on a show in front of the outside world, but on the inside, I was miserable. The decision to slowly dissolve my marriage was made. Nobody seemed to notice.

I began to daydream about my former high school fiancé and sweetheart. Not satisfied with the way my life was turning out, I decided to reach out to Patrick. I thought I needed someone to rescue me from my inner hell. Although I knew it was completely against God's will, as a child of an alcoholic, I leaned into this destructive pattern of adultery, trying to find normal. Trying to find love.

I felt ignored and unloved by my husband. I blamed him for my troubles and my downfalls. I felt as though his drinking had taken my place and I could not compete with it. It always won. We argued about money, jobs, and the kids. I wanted to find unconditional love and support. I knew I needed something I did not have.

I sent the email one afternoon and held my breath.

About ten minutes later, I received an email back.

That day, we started our relationship in our hearts.

From then on, I couldn't think about anything else. I was consumed and my selfishness took over in full swing. After just a few weeks, my husband discovered email exchanges between Patrick and me. I left the next day.

The events of the next few months were both sad and happy. I had what I wanted, but I left a path of destruction behind me. Patrick, also still married at the time, was found out by his family. We created a snowball of emotions and hurt many people along our selfish road to rediscovering each other. We both committed a sin. We both committed adultery. The way we went about starting our relationship is something we regret, but through God's grace we have received forgiveness and healing.

WHERE WAS GOD?

Jail. DUI conviction. Adultery. Another divorce. Who had I become and why? What was causing this out of control behavior? Why had I turned so far away from God after he saved me years prior? The answer is simple really. I started living for self instead of living for him. God didn't leave me when I sat all night in jail—I turned from him before the metal bars clanked shut behind me. God didn't leave me when I suffered through depression and unhappiness—I turned away from him out of my own shame. God didn't leave me when I made the decision to seek another man while still married—I turned away from him and his ways through my adultery. He stood back and watched me err in judgment, like a loving Father, but he allowed me to suffer through the consequences of my actions.

Bad choices such as adultery or even driving while intoxicated are patterns that some adult children of alcoholics repeat. In searching for what normal looks like, many of our decisions are twisted. I've been there. Regret of my DUI and adultery is always there, but I know *all* of my sins are redeemed by God. Only through Jesus' sacrifice on the cross and through God's forgiveness am I truly able to be free from that shame and guilt over these devastating actions.

Our heavenly Father gives us freedom to make our own decisions. What we do with that freedom determines if we are living for ourselves or for him. Because of growing up with an alcoholic parent, my thoughts and actions were tangled. I felt as though I had already messed up and was beyond redemption. While growing up with a parent who drank, if I did something wrong, Dad would stop talking to me and would show his anger openly. In my mind, this is how God viewed my mistakes and bad choices. I figured God felt the same way about me as my dad would.

I actually thought God didn't love me anymore. For many years, the shame and guilt consumed me until I decided I would never be able to have a relationship with him. I had become a bad person. Maybe you have felt this way, too. You are not alone, I can assure you. But I have good news for you—that is not how it works!

- **God loves us regardless of our sins.** *"But God demonstrates His own love toward us, in that while we were yet sinners, Christ died for us."* – **Romans 5:8**
- **God loves us enough to convict (not condemn or judge) our hearts of our sins.** *"'For God did not send the Son into the world to judge the world, but that the world should be saved through Him.'"* – **John 3:17**
- **God loves all of us enough to forgive us of our sins.** *"If we confess our sins, He is faithful and righteous to forgive us our sins and to cleanse us from all unrighteousness."* – **1 John 1:9**
- **God wants all of us to recognize the truth and come back to him.** *"This is good and acceptable in the sight of God our Savior, who desires all men to be saved and to come to the knowledge of the truth."* – **1 Timothy 2:3-4**

So often we allow our past to determine our future. Our path is already determined by God—it is up to us whether we take a detour. He doesn't promise the road he has chosen for us will always be lined with daisies, but he does promise that whoever believes in him shall never perish (John 3:16). For too long, my life seemed as if it had perished. Depression had overcome me and I sought happiness from other people. According to the Merriam-Webster dictionary, in order to be happy one must have a *"feeling* (of) pleasure and enjoyment *because* of your life, situation, etc."* In contrast, joy is "a *source* or *cause* of great happiness." Happiness is temporary, a simple feeling because of your circumstances, but joy is a source. What is your source of joy? I'm talking deep down, in your heart, undeniable joy (Psalm 19:8). I had lost my joy as a result of living in the past— looking backward instead of keeping my eyes pointed toward Jesus.

I have found joy in knowing my heavenly Father sent his only son, Jesus, to earth to die on the cross for my sins (John 3:16). He did this because he wants me—and you—to live in eternity with him. He knew we would fall into sin and need a savior, a rescuer, to help free us from that bondage. I drove a motor vehicle after I drank alcohol—that is a sin (Ephesians 5:18). I committed adultery—that is a sin (Leviticus 20:10). These are some of the shackles of sin that kept me bound for too long. I have been set free by the kindness of my heavenly Father because he loves me enough to forgive me.

According to his word, we are preordained to do great things in his name (Ephesians 2:10). If we choose to follow him, our paths will be straight (Proverbs 3:6). The Bible gives us clear direction when we open our hearts to receive it. Pray and ask Jesus to help you, and he will (Hebrews 4:16). The past is over and the future starts now. It's time to break free from the shackles of the old self and find joy in the freedom of Jesus Christ!

> *Heavenly Father,*
>
> *Please forgive me for living a life full of sin. Many of the choices I make are not choices you would have me make, but you have given me freedom to make my own decisions. Forgive me for using that gift against you. Thank you for sending Jesus to the cross to atone for my sins. I am humbled knowing you are my Father and despite my flaws and bad choices, you love me anyway.*
>
> *In Jesus name,*
>
> *Amen!*

> *It was for freedom that Christ set us free; therefore keep standing firm and do not be subject again to a yoke of slavery.*

Galatians 5:1

Chapter 6
Confessions of an Enabler

Keep watching and praying that you may not enter into temptation; the spirit is willing, but the flesh is weak.

Matthew 26:41

Patrick and I finalized our respective divorces and were dating again after twenty years of being apart. I was truly happy for the first time in years. I thought I had finally found what I had been searching for. Our lives fell back into place, just where we had left off. I felt like a teenager again.

Mom and I rented a small apartment. I bought a new car, and for the first time, began building a new life without anyone's help. I had a good job and enjoyed a sense of accomplishment. Everything I thought I needed lay right before me. Life was good.

Dad floated between relatives over the five years or so he and Mom had been apart. They had not discussed divorce. The love she had for him was just as strong as it had been when they first married and not even addiction could change that.

I spent more time with Patrick than I did with Mom then. We were getting to know each other again. Slowly falling back into place. His divorce went swiftly and amicably. He had been the lucky one between us. He could carry on a civil conversation with his ex-wife, something I had not been able to do with either of my ex-husbands. I had a difficult time understanding this. Why didn't they hate each other? Why didn't they yell and fight over the kids? Why did she *want* to have a conversation with me and get to know me? These questions eluded me for a while. I finally asked Patrick how it was they could talk to each other without an argument ensuing. Although the way our relationship had started was wrong, Patrick and his ex-wife thought it important to remain a solid parental structure for their children. He shared this with me later and I admired them for this. She wanted to get to know me because she knew I would spend time with her children. My respect for her grew when I learned these things.

Shame about the way our relationship began crept in from time to time, but I pushed it aside quickly. I didn't want to confront my guilt. I continued to rationalize my actions by telling myself I deserved to be happy after so many years of misery. This guided my thoughts and decisions. I looked out for myself, something I had never done before. I deserved to have a good life. I deserved to have a life free from drama and chaos. I deserved to have a life where I felt loved and appreciated. Me, me, me. That is what it was all about.

My biological children were adults by the time Patrick and I started dating again. His children were still in school; thirteen and sixteen. They had a difficult time with our relationship. I don't blame them for this. The motives for our relationship were purely selfish. My second ex-husband forbade me from having anything to do with my stepchildren and that crushed me. I knew I would miss out on so many of the important things in their lives, but as Nanny would always say, "You've made your bed, now you have to lie in it." Literally.

§

Dad called one day out of the blue. We had not heard from him in months.

My sister Emily and I wanted to see him, but we were apprehensive. We didn't know what to expect. We didn't have any idea how he lived or what he looked like anymore. My brother-in-law had last seen Dad under a bridge in Dallas as he drove to work. How long had he been homeless? Not having enough to eat, not knowing where he would sleep, not having family near him? Fear and apprehension consumed me. I knew he would be different and I wasn't sure I wanted to see him again. I grappled with so much pain and anger toward him for choosing his alcohol and pills over his family. I couldn't understand what made him want to live the life he lived.

I wrote him many letters in my journal over the years. That was my way of trying to come to terms with his rejection. He was no longer the tower of strength I had always thought. I determined he was a very weak and feebleminded person that only cared about himself. The memories of him preaching to me about the importance of family haunted my mind and heart. Why couldn't he practice what he preached? *What a hypocrite*, I thought.

After much discussion, Emily and I decided to visit him. We prepared ourselves for what we might see and how we would react. Endless possibilities swam around in our minds like water draining from a sink but never emptying completely. Dad gave us his address and we drove there one Saturday morning—just the two of us scared siblings about to face the unknown.

We knew by the address it was a part of Dallas that was not the best, but when we arrived the reality of the situation sank in. We were in one of the seediest areas of Dallas. It was clearly a neighborhood where two young, pretty girls should not be alone. We had the sunshine on our side, but that was it. I pulled into the rundown apartment complex and we sat in my car for a while. I don't know exactly what we thought or how long we sat there, but we finally collected some courage to go up to his apartment.

The complex's dilapidated exterior was covered in faded yellow paint. It looked like a former rent-by-the-hour hotel. We found his apartment. We stood there a moment and took a deep breath, our eyes darting around to make sure nobody followed us or watched us. My heart pounded within the walls of my chest, thumping so rapidly I thought it might crack my breastbone. I slowly raised my hand and knocked on the door.

It took a few minutes for Dad to respond.

"Come in!" We heard him on the other side of the door. His voice sounded raspy.

I opened the door and we filed into the room.

"Mija?"

"Hi, Dad."

He sat in the middle of the open space of the apartment in a recliner. The only other furniture was a small table. It was dark and dirty. The smell of old grime and mouse droppings filled my nostrils. I couldn't tell what color the carpet was because it was so dark. The only light came from the picture window beside the door we had just entered. The sun peeked wearily through several broken slats of the drawn blinds.

I brought pictures so he would have more recent photos of the family. We stood there and talked, explaining the happenings of the last five years we had been apart. He fared rather well holding a conversation; the awkward exchange quickly revealed subtle hints of his old self. Small intricacies of the dad we once knew crept in between moments of slightly normal chatter and his drunken haze. To our disappointment he was obviously still an active alcoholic. Beer cans lay scattered on the floor. I asked if we could look around the apartment and he obliged.

As we walked down the hallway to our right, we entered the bedroom. On the floor was a small pile of urine-infused clothes.

Beside the pile was a pallet where we assumed he slept. Across the hall was a sparse bathroom just a basic washroom with a toilet, sink, and shower. Back down the small hall and past the living room, the kitchen held a dingy refrigerator containing a few staple items—not much to speak of. I opened the stove and the roaches scurried around trying to find a new place to hide. My heart ripped in half at the sights. Over the past few years away from Mom, he had gone from a clean home with the necessities of life and the love of a good woman, to absolute squalor. I couldn't wrap my head around why this was so much more appealing to him, but I made the choice not to ask. It didn't matter anyway, what mattered was we were there and we were going to be Dad's heroes, just like he had been ours when we were young.

"Dad, why don't we run to the store and pick up some things you need?" I said.

He agreed and bent over to put on his shoes. His feet were swollen beyond the point of recognition and for the life of me I don't know how he even used them to walk.

"Here, let me help."

"I got it." He wasn't angry when he said it, but I felt a small twinge of hurt that I quickly decided to release. I wondered if we felt like strangers to him. He certainly felt like a stranger to me.

We made it to the car and he navigated us to the closest store. We purchased a broom, mop, basic cleaning supplies, and several other items he needed. We loaded the car with the provisions and decided to go to the grocery store. Dad had some money left from his disability and we pitched in a little to get him some food. We went back to the apartment and spent the day cleaning and trying to get rid of the houseguests that had invaded the stove and who knew where else.

"Dad, do you want us to help you?" I asked.

"What do you mean? You have helped me today. Thank you, Mija."

"I mean, do you want help like this every month? We could come back and make sure you have paid all of your bills and get groceries when your disability comes in each month."

He sat there for a minute without saying a word.

"We really don't mind helping. We love you," I said.

"If you want to."

"We will come back and help you, but you have to promise that you won't drink when you know we are coming."

"Okay."

"You promise?"

"Okay."

Feeling accomplished, we vowed to come back the next month and told him what day. He wrote it on the small pocket calendar by his chair and we said our goodbyes.

The next month we went back and repeated our heroic efforts. He had kept his promise not to drink and we took him around to pay his bills and get food for the month. The month after that, we took Leah with us so she could see her papa. Now eighteen and a high school graduate; she had been about to enter high school the last time she saw him.

We pulled into the apartment complex and walked up to the door. We had become pros by this time and came prepared with pepper spray in case we were attacked. I knocked on the door and we waited.

Nothing.

I knocked again.

Quiet.

"Dad, you okay?" I knocked again a little harder using the side of my fist so he could hear in case he was still asleep or in the bathroom.

Nothing.

I tried to peer through the broken blinds in an effort to see inside, but it was futile.

I knocked even louder.

"Dad, come to the door!" I yelled this time.

I looked around at Leah and saw the fear in her eyes. Emily just looked defeated. I had visions of him lying on the floor either passed out from an early morning of binge drinking or worse; maybe he was dead.

"What should we do?" Leah asked.

"Maybe we should drive around and see if we can see him somewhere," I said.

So that is what we did. We drove to all the places we had been the month before, hoping we would find him with grocery bags in his hands walking back home. He was nowhere to be found. We drove back to the apartment in one last attempt to find him.

There he was, being helped up the stairs by some man we had never seen before. Dad wasn't walking too steadily and we foolishly thought maybe he had fallen or something. When we got out of the car and made it up to him, the realization slapped me in the face. He was drunk. His effort to be sober when we came the month before was short-lived. He just couldn't do it. He couldn't stay sober long enough to wait for us to come.

"Dad, what are you doing? Where have you been?"

"I didn't think you were coming." He could barely speak coherently.

"Dad, we wrote it on your calendar. Why wouldn't we come?" I said.

"Well, I didn't know."

We took over from the stranger and helped him into the apartment. Leah was close behind us. I was so disappointed and confused. I really thought he was trying, but I was so wrong.

"Dad, we can't keep doing this. I brought your granddaughter today so you could see her, but you can't even see straight."

"Hi, Mija." He smiled up at Leah from his chair and tried to focus on her.

"Hi, Papa," she said, and looked back toward me. I could see disappointment and fear in her eyes.

"Dad, if you are going to continue to drink, we cannot continue to come help you. You made a promise, remember?"

"Yeah."

For the next few minutes, I spoke to him as if he were my child. I repeated my disappointment and frustration.

"Dad, we love you, but we cannot continue like this. This is it. You want your booze more than you want us in your life. I can't take it anymore."

With those words hanging in the air, we left drunken Dad sitting in his recliner in the dilapidated apartment for the last time. Even though we had found him, the Dad we knew was trapped inside the darkness of the disease and, we believed, lost forever.

§

Albert Einstein defined insanity as doing the same thing over and over again and expecting different results. I had no idea I could be defined this way. I left my childhood home because I wanted to be free from living with an alcoholic father. I went from one unhealthy relationship to another. Then I married the absolute love of my life, my high school sweetheart from another time—a time when the whole world was on my horizon. Although the journey to find him again wasn't virtuous by any means, I knew he was the man I was meant to spend the rest of my life with. I had actually known all along. Through the pain of the first marriage and the restlessness of the second, my thoughts always traveled back to Patrick. Our love was so strong that we literally picked right up where I had left it lying on the front porch of my home all those years prior.

We had a small informal ceremony in the backyard of the home we had bought together the month prior. It was early fall and we decided to have a barbeque and invite our family, our children, and Patrick's closest friends from our high school days. Our intent was to surprise everyone with the marriage. Our guests thought we were having a small get-together to celebrate the purchase of our home but we surprised the crowd as the justice of the peace, also a friend, performed the ceremony. Most of them were shocked, but some were not. Our friends and family were happy for us and we were beginning our life together.

The cake had been eaten, the honeymoon was over, and we were starting back to the daily routine. Work, bills, dinners, and grocery store trips kept us busy. My children were grown and his were in high school and lived with their mother, so most of the kids' activities were in the past. We were newlyweds and empty nesters. Mom had stayed with me through everything and she made it her life's mission to take care of us since we worked very hard and made long commutes. She was and is a very good caretaker.

You may be wondering, "How can she live with her mother?" Well, to be perfectly honest, it hasn't always been the easiest thing for me or for her. Mom has a natural instinct to mother me and she tells me that reflex will never go away. I believe it. We have had our words over the years and sometimes they became yelling matches that ended with tears and broken hearts over things that were said— especially when it came to my husband.

"I like my beer," Patrick told me when we dated the second time around.

"Well, okay." I wondered why this comment had come out of the blue. I knew he drank some, but I never noticed him being drunk, so I turned a blind eye to it.

"No one is going to tell me I can't drink. I like having a few beers in the evenings to take the edge off after work. Is that so wrong?"

"Well, I suppose not." His proclamation surprised me, but I let it be.

This marriage actually was so much better than the two that preceded it. My husband loved me very much and I loved him. We took annual vacations together, but aside from that we were homebodies. Well, he was a homebody. Sometimes I wanted to get out of the confines of the house. He spent the weekends sitting on the couch sipping a cold one—or two or three. I spent the weekends shopping. That shopping temporarily filled a need within me—a need to feel worthy, which is common with children of alcoholics. Internally I still longed for something. I had gotten exactly what I had wanted regardless of the impact it left on the people in my life but now that I had it, I still felt empty. I drifted in and out of depression again, constantly hungry for something more, something that would fill the dark space within me.

Shopping seemed to do the trick at least for a little while. Mom and I would be out all day on any given Saturday. We hit almost every store on our trip and I bought something at every stop. I felt fulfilled in the moment. Instant gratification despite the cost, eerily similar to the behavior of an addict.

Around dinnertime we arrived back home and it took fifteen minutes or so to unload the car. In the beginning, my heart raced with apprehension while bringing everything in the house, fearful my husband would be furious with me for spending so much money. That was what I had been used to in the past, but I quickly learned that he didn't care. It didn't bother him in the least. Eventually, I assumed he enjoyed not having me around to bother him about his drinking and napping.

At first I wondered why he didn't want to spend time with me apart from sitting on the couch watching movies. Then I began to make excuses for the drinking. He was just anti-social, he just wanted quiet time after working a stressful job, he is an introvert; the list went on and on. I continually enabled his drinking for fear he would leave me if I created a fuss. I sought advice from family and a few select people I worked with, but I heard things like, "Just do what you want without him," and, "If he truly loved you, he would sacrifice what he wants for what you want." Were those things true?

The answers confused me. Instead of trying to do something about my feelings, I just pushed them down deeper within me. Once again, my world grew darker and darker like storm clouds looming overhead.

After a few years of marriage, I secretly did notice Patrick's drinking becoming more frequent, but I rejected my own instinct to react. I chose to block out what I knew in exchange for enabling him again. My mother, on the other hand, did not reject or block her instincts.

"I'm worried about Patrick," she mentioned as we traveled on another shopping excursion.

"What about?"

"It just seems like he drinks an awful lot."

"Mother, he works hard and is under a lot of stress at work. If he wants to drink a few beers, I don't see anything wrong with that."

"I know, Kim, but he is drinking more and more it seems. I just want him to be healthy."

"Mom, I really don't want to talk about this."

That was it. The conversation was over and Mom knew it. I also realized my secret was not truly a secret. I eventually learned not only was my mother worried about my husband, but his mother was worried about him as well. At times I thought maybe I should be concerned, but then I would reverse my thinking. Instead, I attempted to manage how much he drank. I purchased his beer for him in order to dictate how much he drank. My enabling switched from covering up for his behavior to controlling it. I did this week after week and continued thinking I was doing him a service. Insanity.

One morning I decided to mention something to him, gently.

"Baby, maybe you could slow down just a bit on your drinking." I knew from experience to never speak to an alcoholic while they were drunk. That proved to be more and more difficult as the years went by, so morning was my only option for this conversation.

"What do you mean?"

"Well, I mean, if you could wait until I came home in the evenings, and then have something to drink maybe."

"Why? What difference does it make when I drink?"

"What if I was in a wreck or something? How would you be able to come for me?"

He considered this for a little bit.

"You're right, I could do that. That's a good idea."

He kissed me goodbye and he left for work.

He did really well for a while and then before I knew it, it was back to slurring words when I would call him on my way home from work. Now, I'm not going to sit here as I write these words and tell you that I was little Miss Innocent; I certainly would have a drink here and there. When we were on vacation in Jamaica, I drank mimosas in the morning and then hung out at the swim up bar in the afternoons. I was on vacation. I was supposed to let loose and enjoy the beach, sun, and fun. I didn't know my occasional drinking and enabling his drinking were contributing to his disease. This eventually led to bigger problems in our marriage.

Alcoholism is a cunning and baffling condition. I would learn so much more about it than I ever thought over the next few years. I thought I knew everything there was to know about drinkers. I thought Patrick was different. I was utterly and completely in love with him and believed nothing he could ever do was going to change that. So, I resolved myself to live with it. Accept him for who he was and move on. Get over it. Let him do whatever he wanted to do to his body. It's not mine, right? Meanwhile, I was dying on the inside. The darkness smothered me at times and my emotional health suffered as a result. I was gone from home as much as possible and when I was home, I had my nose stuck in my phone wasting time. Wasting time had become my hobby. I was far from my husband and so far from God that I couldn't tell he had been knocking on my door for years and I had been ignoring Him. I was blind to the insanity of repeating the same actions I had learned growing up with an alcoholic for a father.

Where Was God?

Not surprisingly, I had become an enabler. I allowed, and at times encouraged, Patrick's drinking. Buying beer in an effort to control his intake, drinking with him in hopes he would stop when I did, and keeping my feelings of disdain toward his passed out drunken state buried inside. I didn't realize the patterns I repeated as I attempted to hold on to my marriage. Feelings of shame and guilt as a result of two failed marriages and the fears of losing another loomed over me. I had become smothered in my own misery and didn't realize it. So where was God in all of this misery? Doesn't he want us to be joyful? Yes, that is true, he does, but when we turn away from his guidance and will for our lives, we allow Satan to interfere and begin the slow ruin of our souls.

We are weak by nature. The Lord our God made us that way. He wants us to depend on him and not on ourselves. Jesus tells us in Matthew 26:41, *"'Keep watching and praying that you may not enter into temptation; the spirit is willing, but the flesh is weak.'"* Our flesh is weak and in order to prevent us from falling from God's sweet grace, we have to be alert and aware of Satan's ploys. 1 Peter 5:8 warns us, *"Be of sober spirit, be on the alert. Your adversary, the devil, prowls around like a roaring lion, seeking someone to devour."* Our enemy is waiting for us.

- Satan wants us in our weakest state.
- Satan preys on us when we are vulnerable.
- Satan desires us to move farther away from God's presence.
- Satan feeds his evilness with our failings.
- Satan delights in reminding us of our shortcomings.

God, on the other hand, only wants what is best for us. He is a loving Father who is looking out for his children's best interests.

- *"But as many as received Him, to them He gave the right to become children of God, even to those who believe in His name."* – **John 1:12**

- *"The Spirit Himself testifies with our spirit that we are children of God."* – **Romans 8:16**

- *"Therefore be imitators of God, as beloved children."* – **Ephesians 5:1**

We should apply purpose in our lives that includes doing what is true, honorable, just, pure, lovely, and commendable (Philippians 4:8). God gives us the instruction in his Word. Only by staying close to him, am I able to know how to handle any situation that may arise. There will be times of struggle, but in those times I shouldn't stick my head in the sand and hope the battle will go away on its own. God only wants the best for us through difficult times. He is forever faithful. I have to remember to turn to him first and then talk to my family—openly and honestly. I must set healthy boundaries of what I will tolerate and what I will not tolerate. These boundaries remind me and those around me that I will not enable negative behavior. I have choices. Through the strength of the Holy Spirit within, Satan has no control over me or my choices.

- *"Devise a plan, but it will be thwarted; State a proposal, but it will not stand, For God is with us."* – **Isaiah 8:10**

- *"But you, O Lord, are a God merciful and gracious, Slow to anger and abundant in lovingkindness and truth."* – **Psalm 86:15**

- *"Know therefore that the LORD your God, He is God, the faithful God, who keeps His covenant and His lovingkindness to a thousandth generation with those who love him and keep his commandments."* – **Deuteronomy 7:9**

I wish I had known Father God then like I do now. If I had had a relationship with him, things would have been different. Through the revelation of God's Spirit I am able to recognize the devil's schemes. The darts of doubt that threaten my mind can be deflected using my shield of faith (Ephesians 6:16). His lies can be smothered by tightening the belt of truth (Ephesians 6:14).

I am no longer ashamed of my past because I know my heavenly Father loves me unconditionally. I am forgiven by a sovereign, loving God. Satan tries to remind me of previous thoughts, feelings, and actions, but he is no match for Father God. With God's help, I know the importance of setting boundaries lovingly, I understand what enabling behavior looks like, and I am no longer fearful of my life ending with regrets.

> *Finally, brethren, whatever is true, whatever is honorable, whatever is right, whatever is pure, whatever is lovely, whatever is of good repute, if there is any excellence and if anything worthy of praise, dwell on these things.*

Philippians 4:8

Chapter 7
Home at Last

*But we had to celebrate and rejoice, because this brother of
yours was dead and has begun to live, he was lost and has
been found.*

Luke 15:32

Isn't it strange how life can coast along, everything moving in one
perpetual motion, and then suddenly the boat capsizes? The life you
once knew is floating aimlessly around you. Nothing can be done,
you are completely helpless, and there is no hope to be found. That
is how I felt after the phone rang one day. Up until then I led a fairly
well ordered, ordinary existence. Nothing special. Then out of
nowhere an unexpected life speeding uncontrollably toward me,
crashed and left behind a pile of rubble.

"We found Papa," my daughter Leah said when I picked up the
phone as I drove home from work.

"Where?" My first thought was that he had turned up dead somewhere. We had not seen Dad in over five years and weren't sure where he had been all of that time. We knew he lived under bridges more often than not, but over the last year or so, nobody had heard anything about him.

"He's in the hospital."

"What happened?" My heart pounded and my thoughts raced.

"We're not completely sure." She became quiet for a moment, then added, "I'm going to see him, Momma."

I wasn't sure what to say. Fear set in. Fear that Leah would be disappointed and hurt when she saw him. Since I hadn't seen or heard from Dad in so long, I didn't know what to expect.

"Is Auntie going too?"

"I don't know yet, but I need to go." She was crying now.

I thought for a few moments. The red light changed to green. A horn honked urging me to go. I pressed on the gas pedal.

"Okay, I'm going with you."

Just like that, in a split second without giving it another thought, I decided to see my father again. Although I knew I needed to do it, a tornado of emotions swirled around me. I arrived home to pick up Leah and discovered Mom was determined to go with us. Everything happened so quickly. It seemed like seconds flew by before we walked into the hospital elevator. None of us knew what to expect when we saw him. We braced ourselves and knocked on the door of his room.

"Come in." His voice was the same, just raspier than I remembered.

The four of us filed in. I do not remember who led the way, but he sat on the side of the bed and slowly raised his head. I smiled as if the past few years had not existed.

"Hi, Mija." He laughed softly, maybe out of nervousness mixed with happiness. It had been a very long time for him too.

"Hi, Dad," I said.

When he laid eyes on Mom it was like no time had passed between them. She walked over to him—her hands shook—and they kissed. I was shocked by this display. I didn't expect them to just fall right back to the way things were before. We sat and talked for a long time about life, kids, work, and marriages. My marriages mostly.

"Who are you married to now?" Dad asked.

"Patrick."

"Well, it's about time!" He laughed.

"I know it really is. We've been married for almost five years now."

"That's good, that's good. He's a good man?"

"Yes, he is."

"Well, he always was."

We found out Dad had fallen and broken his hip. He lived with some friends of his who had brought him to the hospital a couple days after he fell. The doctors repaired his hip and he had been recovering for about two weeks, but at this point there was no sign of the so-called friends. While in the hospital, the doctors discovered stomach cancer. After years of abusing his body with alcohol and prescription painkillers, I assumed he would eventually die of cirrhosis of the liver or something similar, but not cancer. We were shocked by this revelation.

"So what are the doctors going to do?" I asked.

"They want to do surgery, but I don't want it. I don't want to be cut on again."

"But Dad, what if they can help you?"

"I don't have anything to live for, Mija."

Of course he thought that. He had lost his family long ago. I walked away years before. I couldn't blame him for feeling as though there was nothing left to live for.

"Dad, you have to have the surgery. You have to let them try."

He considered this for a few minutes, looking around the room at each one of us.

"Dad, you have us now. We are here for you."

"I'll think about it."

We were with Dad for about three hours, but it seemed as though time stood still. Everything fell back into place. *Maybe we really could help him now*, I thought. *Maybe there is hope.*

Dad had been a smoker my entire life. He was bent on us taking him in the wheelchair downstairs so he could smoke, so we loaded up his six-foot-plus lankiness and headed out. I pushed him to the elevator. The doors slid open and I rolled him in. He sat silent in the wheelchair on the way down. Even though it was past seven in the evening, the scorching Texas heat stole our breath. We wheeled Dad out the sliding doors and searched for a safe place to park. We figured out after watching a few others the sidewalk beside the busy street was the place to be.

"Man, it's hot out here today!" I said.

"It sure is," Dad said.

We talked about the weather, Dad and I smoked, Emily and Leah watched us. After over five years of not seeing or hearing anything from him, all we managed to talk about was the weather. It was surreal.

Dad smoked three cigarettes. We made our way back up to his room, stayed through dinner, and decided it was time to leave. We hated the thought of leaving him there by himself. I don't know why really, he had been on his own in much worse conditions than a hospital. Deplorable conditions, I'm certain of it. Maybe we felt if we left him he wouldn't be there when we came back the next day. Maybe we felt like this was all a dream and if we left, it would force us to wake up and it would be over. Maybe we felt like once he had some sleep, he would realize he didn't really want to see us anymore. Maybe it was all of those feelings and more stirring around in our minds. I know they were stirring in mine.

"We'll be back in the morning, Dad, okay?" I told him.

"Okay, Mija. I'll be here." He laughed a little when he said it.

We each kissed him before we left. During the drive home we chattered about the unbelievable events of the day. We discussed different feelings and the possibilities of what would come of this reunion. We truly didn't know, but decided to take it one day at a time.

The next morning, we coordinated our planned meeting time and traveled back to the hospital. We arrived around breakfast.

"I'm sick of drinking my food. I want real food!"

We could tell his mood had shifted.

"What did you have?" I asked.

"Broth. Blah!" he said, as he childishly stuck his tongue out.

"Have you seen the doctor yet this morning?"

"Not yet."

"Well, maybe when he comes in we can ask him if you can have some real food."

"I doubt it."

"Have you decided what you are going to do about the surgery?" I asked.

"Yeah, I have."

"Well?"

"I'm going to have it. I have something to live for now. I have all of you back."

"I'm so happy! You made the right decision, Dad!"

We were happy, but still needed answers. I wanted to talk to the doctor myself and find out exactly how bad the stomach cancer was. Emily and Mom felt the same way. We spent a few hours hanging out with Dad and catching up on the past few years. Mom sat right by him and they held hands the entire time.

"Good morning, Mr. Guerra," the doctor said as he came in the room.

"Morning."

"How are you feeling this morning?"

"I want some food."

"Did you not have breakfast this morning?"

"No, I had liquid. I want real food."

"Well now, we are going to have to talk more about that later."

"What's wrong with right now?"

"I need to know if you are sure you don't want the surgery. That is my first priority right now. When we talked last you just wanted to go home. Is that still the case?" He looked around the room at each of us. We had made our introductions to him the evening before. He had been pleased to know Dad's family was around him, and I think he secretly came back in that morning asking about the surgery because we were there.

"I'm ready to have it. When can we do it?"

"I'm happy to hear that. We can schedule for tomorrow morning, bright and early."

"Good, now that's settled. When can I eat?"

"Wait, Dad. Doctor, we would like more information about this surgery, please," Emily said.

"Your dad has stomach cancer. We don't know what stage it is and we won't until we attempt to remove the mass. On the last film, it looked like it was only in his stomach, but it's difficult to tell until we go in there."

"Dad, are you certain you want to have the surgery? We don't want you to do anything you don't want to do. It's all up to you," Emily said.

He sat there a few moments thinking, looked at us, and then answered, "Yes. I have my family back and I want to spend as much time as I can with them. Let's do it."

With that settled, the doctor left and we decided to grab something to eat ourselves. By the time we returned, my grandma and aunt, Dad's mom and sister, were there visiting. Grandma cried a lot and that irritated Dad. He always hated to see women cry, especially those he loved.

The rest of the day relatives came in and out. We meandered about the hospital when he had visitors, mainly because we didn't know who they all were. Dad came from a huge Hispanic family, so there were more cousins than I could count using my fingers and toes.

"Who was that?" I asked after I passed a woman and man leaving as I was coming back in.

He shrugged his shoulders and we laughed about it.

"I don't remember who some of these people are. Some of them I haven't seen since I was a kid. Why are they all coming around now?"

I recognized a few of his favorite cousins. He was so happy to see them, too. They grew up together and kept in touch off and on throughout their adult life. Just like us, they hadn't seen Dad or heard where he was in the last five years or so. There was one cousin—one as close as a brother—that would not be able to come see him. We hadn't gathered enough courage to tell him. It would be the most difficult news to share. Out of all of the catching up we had done, we had avoided that topic. Until all of the visitors had left and Dad's dinner of another round of broth had been delivered and rejected.

"Dad, we need to talk to you about something."

"Okay."

"It's about Herman."

"Where is Herman these days?"

Mom took the lead. "Herman died last year, honey." Tears welled up in her eyes.

He sat silent for a minute letting the news soak in. "Oh man. Really? I can't believe it." He tilted his head down and stared at his feet. "What happened?"

"He had pancreatic cancer. He didn't tell anyone. We didn't even know he had been sick. It happened real fast."

"I was supposed to go before he did. He always took such good care of himself." He couldn't look up at us. He was lost in his own thoughts and we could tell he had a lump stuck in his throat.

"You okay?" I asked.

"Yeah, I'll be fine. I just can't believe it."

Honestly, I had a difficult time believing any of the events that were happening. It seemed more like a dream; a very long dream. I wished for so many years Dad would get better and want to be around us. I had longed for the family we had when I was younger. Now that dream was a reality, but it still didn't feel real.

After discussing it, we decided I would stay the first night with him. We didn't want to leave him alone with his thoughts and I was looking forward to some one-on-one time with him. Everyone stayed until visiting hours were over and by that time it was late and I was exhausted. We talked for a little while, but he really needed his rest for the surgery the next day. I knew he was nervous, although he tried hard not to let it show. I was nervous too. As I lay there on the stiff hospital cot beside his bed, I looked at the night sky. I whispered a small prayer that God would keep Dad safe the next day; the most I had talked to God in a very long time. The darkness of my heart, though, was just beginning to creep in.

§

We woke early the next morning. Since Dad's surgery was scheduled for nine, all he could have was black coffee or water. Of course, he wanted a smoke first thing. I got him in his chair and we strolled downstairs to the sidewalk that had become our spot. I could tell he was nervous about what the next few hours would hold, but he was still trying hard to conceal it.

As the sun broke through the overcast sky, I wheeled him back to the elevator and up we went to sit in his room. We were quiet that morning, not much to talk about, except how much he wanted real food. He was always a big eater and it bothered him because he couldn't have anything of substance. Emily, Leah, and Mom arrived pretty early that morning. We sat waiting for the staff to come get him for the surgery. Mom helped him get a sponge bath. The rest of us went to the cafeteria to get coffee. Tension was very high because none of us knew what to expect. Concerns of him dying on the table covered us like dark clouds coming in before a dreadful storm.

We went back up and noticed some of the staff headed toward the room where Dad sat on the edge of the bed waiting impatiently. I'm sure he had thousands of thoughts spinning around in his mind, too, but he never mentioned what they were. He did his best to climb up on the transport stretcher and off we trailed like ducklings following their mother. We rode the elevator and Dad joked around with the orderlies on the way to his unknown fate. Arriving at our destination, we surrounded him with love and watched him disappear behind the operating room doors. He smiled at us before they swung closed.

Then the waiting.

Not knowing exactly how long the surgery would take, we sat in the community waiting room with another family. We cried, wrung our fingers, rubbed our foreheads and necks; waiting. The doctor had explained that the surgery would take approximately two to three hours. At least that is what he thought.

I heard the door clack open and lifted my head to see Dad's doctor walking in the room, still in his protective operating garb. This isn't right, it's been less than an hour since we loved on him, I thought. It's been less than an hour since I saw him smile at me before the doors shut separating us. Why is he here already? Emily and I looked at each other and stood up to face the doctor.

"He's fine, he's resting now."

"What does that mean?"

"Your dad's cancer is worse than we thought."

"And?" I asked.

"And, well," he stated as he rubbed his forehead, "there isn't anything we can do. It has spread to . . ."

That was all I heard, the rest of his words were a blur. I could hear my mom and aunt crying in the background. I fell into the chair behind me. As he talked, it sounded more like garbled mumbles instead of a man's voice. I saw him turn and walk out. I sat there for a few minutes, but it seemed like hours. I grabbed my purse and shot out of the waiting room. Years of emotions and guilt flowed from my heart and my eyes. I looked around, completely lost to my surroundings. I didn't know where to go—I had to get out of that place. I needed air, hot or not, I didn't care. I heard Emily and Leah behind me. I don't remember what they said. I needed out.

When horrifying things happen, some people lash out, some people cry and scream, some people are silent with their own thoughts, some people are numb, some people pray. I started my withdrawn descent into darkness at full force that morning. I buried my feelings, as I often did then, telling myself I had to remain the strong one for the rest of the family. I needed to always be the tough one and not let my emotions take over. Keeping it together because everyone around me was such a mess, pushing my feelings and emotions down into the depths of my being, exactly where Satan wanted them to go. Although I allowed myself to cry for the first time in years, it only lasted a few minutes. I was much too restrained to allow myself to cry, especially in front of others.

I found myself downstairs on the sidewalk, at "our spot." I pulled out a cigarette and felt Leah and Emily there with me even though I didn't acknowledge them. They knew just to let me be and I thank them for that. Finally, I straightened up as quickly as a snap of two fingers and turned to look at them. I had stopped crying and was done with my cigarette. That's how I operate. I process emotions for a short while and then immediately throw myself into action mode.

"What exactly did the doctor say?" I asked.

They told me the words that I didn't hear earlier. Dad's cancer was much worse than the doctor thought; it had spread to other parts of his digestive system and he likely had about a month to live. One month. Of course they really didn't know. They were just taking an educated guess. They had inserted a tube into his stomach to relieve pressure. It was sort of like a feeding tube, but he would not be eating through it. I didn't quite understand all of this at the time, but I would quickly learn. The doctor would release him on hospice the following day. There was nothing to do but make him comfortable.

"Well then. What do we do?" I looked expectantly at them both. They looked back at me, simply blinking. "Where is he going to go?" I asked.

We decided to each call our husbands. I reached for my cell phone to dial Patrick, and Emily grabbed hers and called her husband. Leah just waited, watching us both as we talked on our phones.

"Dad's not doing well at all. They are going to release him on hospice tomorrow."

"Well, baby, what needs to happen next?"

"I think he should come to our house. I think he would want to be close to Mom. We are going to ask him, of course, and Mom, but I think that would be best."

"I think that's a good decision. How long does he have?"

I struggled a moment to get those words to transfer from my mind and out my mouth.

"About a month."

My husband was quiet for a moment. "Then I will start getting a space ready for him."

"Thank you."

"Of course, baby."

We ended our call and Emily was still on the phone. I had no idea what the future was going to hold for any of us. Everything changed so quickly. One minute I was at work doing my thing, the next I was preparing to bring my estranged dad to my home on hospice care. Strange how God works sometimes.

"He said Dad can move in with us," Emily reported.

"Patrick said the same thing."

Mom and dad's sister agreed it would be best if he came to live with one of us. Now we needed to talk to Dad about it and see what he wanted to do. It was his life, after all, but there we were plotting it all out for him. He was still an adult and was not incapacitated. He was still recovering from the surgery, so we began to wait.

Sitting around a drab hospital is not fun, especially when you are waiting on a loved one that will be gone in a few short weeks. I think somewhere deep down, I hoped that the doctors were wrong and Dad would be back to the strong, loving man I remembered from my childhood. There was too much time to contemplate, to remember, to hope. I wanted desperately to erase the last twenty years of life, except for my kids, and try again. Wipe the slate clean and be in a different situation. I wanted Dad to be the same person he was then. I wanted Mom to be the same woman she once had been. I wanted to be the same innocent, wide-eyed girl looking forward to an exciting life. I had a lot of time to think that day, but the days that followed passed by in a blur.

Dad was settled back in his room and they were making him comfortable with medicine. We decided Emily and Leah would stay the night with him. I had a lot to do at work to prepare for the days and weeks to come. Emily did as well, but I had stayed the night before and was exhausted.

We entered the grim room. He dosed off and on. I don't remember who spoke first once he stirred. One of us let him know that he was going to be released the next day.

"Dad, we want to know where you would like to go," I said.

He looked over at Mom. "I want to be with your mom."

She reached for him and looked down at his large, weathered hands.

"Okay, Mom lives with me. I have a room we don't use. We will fix that one up for you. It doesn't have a door on it, it is a formal dining room that we just use as a sitting area, but we can put the bed in there and the television for you."

"Why can't I sleep with your mom?" He looked at her.

"Honey, they are giving you a bed. An electric one so you can lift up your head anytime you want."

"I'd rather sleep next to you."

"I know, I would too, but you have that tube. I don't think either of us would be very comfortable, do you?" She fought back the tears that threatened.

"Oh yeah." He switched his gaze toward the window beside his bed.

"It'll be okay, Dad. We will make everything comfortable for you. We can probably even move a DVD player in there. We have a ton of movies. You and Patrick have the same taste in movies."

He chuckled halfheartedly, and shifting his gaze from mom's pained face to the blazing Texas sky outside the window.

I wondered what he thought in those moments of stillness. Was he crying on the inside because he desperately wanted to be close to Mom again? Was his heart filled with regret for all of the wasted years? Was he furious with God for taking his life from him slowly? Was he selfishly wishing he had more time to do the things he always wanted to do? I'll never know what was running through his mind that day or the days that followed. It was likely a combination of all those regrets. But while I was seeking to understand his turmoil, the enemy began to subtly suffocate me with the burden of my past. Darkness slowly began to impede upon my heart like a heavy storm moving across the horizon.

§

We spent most of the next day in preparation for the new houseguest. Emily and I conferred in detail with Dad and the hospice representative. Patrick and Leah worked diligently getting the small room ready for Dad's bed and television. Mom spent a lot of time pacing and sitting next to Dad. He was getting irritable and wanted to leave the hospital as swiftly as we could make it happen. Several phone calls and discussions determined when everything would take place. Coordination of an ambulance for transport along with when the hospice equipment would arrive, who would be there to assist the delivery crew, and what the heck was to happen with that tube once we arrived.

The nurses would not allow Dad to eat a bite and they urged us against giving him any food either. They told us the food would get stuck in the tube. The doctor had rerouted everything to exit that darned tube.

"So how is he supposed to get any nutrition?" I asked one of the nurses.

"That's up to the doctor and hospice to figure out. I'm telling you right now, do not let him eat a bite or he will be right back here." She turned on her heels and out the door she went.

We did our best to keep Dad calm, but between the different medication and the fact he loved food almost as much as he loved my mother, he was becoming quite the grouch.

"When can I go home?" he stressed each syllable of the sentence, his eyes set and angry.

"Dad, we are working on it as fast as we can. Please be patient."

"I need to eat. I haven't had anything to eat since yesterday."

"Well, they are telling us you can't eat right now, because they are trying to get you ready to leave." I knew that was a small lie, but I was desperate to pacify him at least for a little while.

"Bull."

Oh boy, he was severely agitated. Nobody came between Dad and his food. Some things never change. Now, he was a good man, don't get me wrong, but sometimes, when he was angry or upset, his looks and words could cut a hole right through you.

After hours of trying to appease Dad and coordinating all of the moving parts of bringing someone home on hospice, Emily and I finally relaxed a little when the ambulance drivers came into the room with a stretcher.

Our stubborn dad tried to get onto that stretcher by himself. He was still recovering from broken hip surgery only two weeks before and had had his stomach filleted open the morning before, but he attempted to move himself. That little exchange should have been a glaring warning to me that things were about to get very interesting in my house.

Finally, he allowed the drivers to do the maneuvering and off we went—Dad to his chariot and Emily and me to my car. We notified home to let them know we would be arriving in about thirty minutes and to be ready. We also warned of Dad's mood. A cyclone of emotions threatened my sister and me, but we pushed back the tears and the racing hearts. We had a job to do.

§

The first thing Dad wanted to do upon arriving at my house was smoke. Smoking in the house was off limits and since he couldn't walk, the wheelchair was the only way to go. He didn't like the idea at first, but quickly realized that being wheeled out to the garage was the only way to get his fix, so he conceded.

The first afternoon was awkward for us. We didn't really know what to say or how to act. The hospice nurse had arrived and Emily, Mom, and I sat around our dining table to discuss all of the events that would be occurring during his stay. It almost sounded like he was at a temporary hotel and soon would be going to some other place. I remember thinking how odd it was to hear the nurse talking. Here this stranger was in my home explaining how the last days of Dad's life were going to be handled by them and what we should do as well.

"Okay, do you have any questions?" the kind blonde nurse asked.

Of course we had questions, but she couldn't answer the most important one—exactly how much time we had left with him. We asked about the medication schedule, what we should do to keep him comfortable, what problems we needed to watch for and of course, food. That was the most important item on the list.

"Can he eat regular food?"

"Give him whatever he wants."

Absolutely we would. Now we had the green light to give him food, we would be crowned as heroes in his mind. I was sure of it.

"Thank God!" we said in unison.

We got a chuckle out of that and so did Dad once he found out what was said. We prepared a list of all of the food he wanted. Patrick went to the grocery store and came back with sacks full of food just for Dad: Salisbury steak, egg rolls, popsicles, and watermelon, just to name a few. Watermelon was the most important staple in Dad's diet. I remember him going to the grocery store multiple times each summer and stepping through the door with two huge watermelons stuck under each arm. He would eat half a watermelon in one sitting. He always had a voracious appetite and loved to cook and loved to eat. It amazed me how he stayed so thin. He was not skinny when I was young, but he was never overweight. Now he was simply becoming gaunt and boney.

After cooking his first meal, one of us delivered food to his bed. He sat up watching a movie on television and ate like he had never eaten before. He was like a youngster again. Like old times, really. Just like I remembered. Patrick had moved Mom's recliner in the room beside the bed and she sat with him while he ate. He enjoyed that food so much as it was going down, relishing every bit, but as soon as he took the last bite, it all came back up. We truly didn't realize until that moment that he couldn't eat a big meal. Luckily it was only soup and watermelon, but even that had been too much.

That was hour one of many more spent helping Dad with his blue emesis bags. Those blue bags became a security blanket for us. Every time Dad would eat, he had a bag close by. Anytime one of us would take him out to the garage to smoke, he had his blue bag. He needed them every single time.

Once bedtime rolled around, we were all depleted and needed some rest. I had decided to work from home the next day so I could help Mom. She decided to sleep in her chair in the small room with Dad. When I finally rested my head on my pillow, my mind battled with itself for sleep. I couldn't shut off the thoughts that circled like the eye of a hurricane. The room was completely dark and my husband was snoring, but my eyes were wide open turning events over and over. Even through this obvious struggle, it did not occur to me to say one word to God about it all.

Dad's days and mine began with coffee, the blue bag, a few smokes, a ride in the wheelchair, back to bed, medicine, the blue bag again, and repeat as needed. I worked from home as much as I could and was so grateful for the ability to do that. Having an understanding employer is a priceless gift during times of suffering. In between business phone calls and emails, Mom needed help getting Dad into the chair to take a short stroll to the garage. It was so incredibly hot, but Dad didn't care. He just wanted to smoke and look outside. Mom would hover a little, out of love and compassion, but still hovering. It would annoy him, but she didn't care. She had been without him for so long, I'm sure she felt as though she needed to do it to show that she really did still love him despite the separation. It irritated Dad, but then again, many things did. He was taking so much medication and I am sure that most of it had side effects of irritability.

Dad knew he was dying, although he didn't talk about it. He and Mom looked through photo albums and she talked about all of the things she had experienced living with me—the time I took her to Las Vegas on a business trip, the concerts she had been to, reconnecting with her best friend from high school, and her volunteering at a local elementary school. Her life had been exciting since he had been gone. Dad's life, on the other hand, had been eventful, just not events that he could share with a smile on his face. He had been wandering around the streets searching for somewhere to lay his head, trying to stay warm during the cold nights, looking for a free, hot meal, and of course, seeking a way to be free from the pain of addiction.

I didn't understand it at all. Just stop. Easy. Done. Over. Well, it's not that easy at all, I would later learn. Addiction is also like a sort of cancer or any other type of disease. The thing with addiction is, once someone who has the tendency or allergy takes the first pain pill or swallows the first drink, that's it. That is all it takes for the dependency to begin. That one innocent pill after a surgery or that one drink at a party with friends and the person is hooked for life. That was Dad. He was hooked for life. The spiral starts slowly, but once it begins, it's like a tornado picking up speed across a barren landscape. Slowly picking up debris and slinging it to a neighboring town five or more miles away. Once the twister has ripped its way through, there is nothing left behind but memories. That is addiction.

Dad had wonderful memories of his family and we would sit in the garage during those precious smoke breaks and talk about them all.

"What are you thinking about, Dad?"

He chuckled. "Just remembering going to my grandma's while Mom went to work."

"Tell me about it."

"My grandma loved having us at her house. She woke up early, around three o'clock in the morning, and started making tortillas and other stuff for us to eat."

"How many of you would go there?"

"Oh gosh, I don't remember exactly, probably around ten of us. A house full of cousins. We had a lot of good times there."

Dad was reflecting on his life every second of every day, I'm sure of it. He shared some moments with me, and others he kept to himself. I wondered how much regret he had. I wondered if he was sad about how his life had turned out, or if the last few years didn't matter anymore because he was finally home. I never asked him.

Maybe I was afraid of the answer. I had my own visions floating in my mind of the things he had endured over the years. These thoughts surfaced every time I looked at him. Although he was skinny and pale from the cancer, I could see the pain of his soul in his eyes. He would get lost looking out of the open garage door watching the bunnies hop around the yard in the mornings. He received so much joy from something so simple and sweet. I looked forward to those early morning quiet times in the garage with him. Sipping on our coffee together, not saying a word, just enjoying each other's company after over five years of being away from each other. I cherished those moments, not knowing how many of them I had left. I'm sure he did too.

I could feel the tension hanging heavy in the house during the first week Dad was there. We were trying everything we could to make him comfortable and happy, overcompensating like one week of TLC was going to make up for years of ignoring him. It was laughable to me and I wondered if he thought the same thing. Again, I didn't ask. I didn't want to know the answer. I knew that we did what we needed to do and I'm sure he knew it too, but the guilt lurked around nonetheless. We were all very tired and sleep was a commodity in short supply. Working full time and then coming home to help Mom take care of Dad was already beginning to take a toll on me. Mom would get frustrated with his stubbornness and he would get frustrated with her mothering him. There was stiffness in the house that wasn't there before. Cancer made everyone's world turn topsy-turvy. We knew he was where he belonged, but even that knowledge didn't help alleviate the stress.

Once I finally found rest at night, the alarm clock took it away too quickly. At times my slumber was interrupted by the sound of my mother crying out in desperation.

"Kimberly!"

I must be dreaming.

"Kimberly!" Mom opened the door to my bedroom.

"Huh?" I was not clear what was happening.

"Get up, Dad fell!" she yelled.

Dad had decided to get out of bed in the early morning hours and go to the bathroom. The problem was, he couldn't walk and at night we raised the bed up so Mom didn't have to bend over to tend to his tube. I jumped up and grabbed my robe, threw it on in a frenzy, and raced out of the bedroom. There he was, sitting up straight on the floor of the hallway beside his bed with stomach juices pouring out of the open hole in his abdomen. The tube had come out completely. My eyes darted to the bed. Just as I suspected, there the tube lay in a brown mess. *Oh brother*, I thought.

"Dad, what happened?" I asked. "Call 9-1-1!" I yelled to Patrick.

"I needed to go to the bathroom."

"Why didn't you wake Mom up?" I asked him. "Mom, call Emily."

"I didn't want to wake her. I can do it by myself," he said.

"Well, obviously you can't. Dad, you can't walk, remember."

"I can do whatever I want to do!" he yelled as he tried to get up.

"Just sit still, Dad."

"Why?" He stopped and looked up at me.

"Because we have to wait for the ambulance."

"What for?"

"Dad, you pulled out your tube!"

"Oh brother." He looked down and realized what happened.

Mom was crying, but we managed to get Dad on a stool so he would be a little more comfortable. The paramedics arrived and Emily and I jumped in the car all within about twenty minutes. In another thirty minutes we were sitting in the hospital emergency room.

I don't think it was until that moment that the events of the past few weeks finally sunk in for Dad. Until then, he had just been in the hospital, no big deal; been reunited with his long lost family, excellent; and he had cancer, no problem. But once he was in the hospital again and this time it was an emergency situation, his view shifted. It was becoming a reality that he would not be alive for long and for just how long, none of us knew.

"I need to get out of here," he said angrily.

"Where are you going to go?"

Emily left the room. Exhaustion and anxiety were winning.

"Home. Get my clothes."

"Dad, you can't leave yet."

"Watch me." His eyes were filling with fury.

"Dad, you can't leave. How are you going to get home? I can't get you in my car."

"I'll take a cab or a bus."

"You can't walk, remember?" I was beginning to show my frustration and fatigue.

He just looked away from me.

"Let's see if we can't get you fixed up," the doctor said as he entered the room.

"Why don't you get me out of here."

"That's exactly what we are trying to do." The doctor was busy fiddling with the stomach wound, and not too gingerly, which was irritating him even more.

I rose to attempt to help the doctor.

"Get. Away. From. Me." I had not seen that look of disdain in dad's eyes since I left home as a teen. I sat in the chair and turned away from him and choked back the giant lump forming in my throat. Finally, I broke down.

Not much can cause me to cry. I think I cried so much during the first eleven years of my adult life, all of my tears dried up. That night, however, the contempt and anger in Dad's eyes brought the flood. It broke my worn out heart.

The doctor had done the best he could to repair the mess and left the room to prepare the discharge papers. The quiet hung in the room for a long while before I finally spoke.

"Dad, you don't have to be so hateful. I'm doing the best I can you know. I don't know what you expect of me."

"I'm. Dying," he hissed through pursed lips.

His words cut me to the core.

That's it. He gets it. He is dying. That was the first time I heard him say it out loud.

"I know, Dad. I love you, but I'm not going to put up with you talking to me like that. I'm—we are all trying to help you." I was not the timid teenager he could say ugly things to anymore. I knew it was important to set the boundaries with him.

We did not speak another word that night. Emotions were simply too raw. We were tired and hurting, but it wasn't until then I realized I really had it easy. I wasn't the one dying.

Cancer is an ugly disease. It takes every ounce of dignity, every smidgen of rest, and each moment of peace, and replaces them with embarrassment, exhaustion, and strife. This happens to the people caring for the sick and more so for the sick themselves. They lose control over bodily functions and pain is unimaginable. The first two weeks were stressful for us, but the days to come would test my family in ways we could have never believed possible.

WHERE WAS GOD?

Why does God allow bad things to happen? This is a question that has been asked for centuries and will continue to be asked until Jesus returns. So many people suffer from the repulsive disease of cancer. It comes in many forms and attacks different parts of the body. According to the American Cancer Society, over one million new cases are reported each year. Where is God in all of this and why does he allow suffering?

After Dad died, I yelled to God, demanding answers. Why did God send Dad back to us, only to take him away under horrible circumstances? Why did God allow Dad to suffer such a painful death? Why did God allow Dad to be an alcoholic? I didn't hear audible responses to my questions. Instead he drew me to the Bible. I searched for answers and came upon these truths.

- *'For as the heavens are higher than the earth, so are My ways higher than your ways and My thoughts than your thoughts.* – **Isaiah 55:9**

- *And we know that God causes all things to work together for good to those who love God, to those who are called according to His purpose.* – **Romans 8:28**

I am not meant to understand God's ways. That is why he is God and I am not. He does things according to his will and purposes. Does this mean I have to be happy every second and through all bad things that happen? No, absolutely not. He understands our sufferings. Remember, he sent Jesus, his son, to earth to dwell among us as a man (John 1:14).

Jesus experienced the same things we experience throughout our lives.

- He was betrayed by his disciples, (Judas and Peter).
- He was abandoned by his disciples.
- He was falsely accused and rejected by the Jewish leaders.
- He carried the burdens of the world's sin, which we are unable to do without Jesus.

My dad was an alcoholic and an addict. God gave him the freedom to choose what path in life he would take. God wanted him, as he wants us, to choose the right path—the path of righteousness. Instead of turning to God when he felt the desire to drink, Dad succumbed to the addiction. As a result of his choices, his disease intensified and caused great loss and destruction. His alcoholism grew into an addiction to pain medication. Ultimately, he lost his home, his family, and his spirit.

During the span when we were estranged, Dad lived on various couches, under bridges, on park benches, in homeless shelters, and in stranger's extra bedrooms. Although a fall led to a broken hip that led to the diagnosis of the stomach cancer, that fall was a blessing in disguise. God didn't want Dad to reach the end of his life alone on a stranger's couch or under a bridge in the stifling heat. God didn't want his family to feel the pain of finding out Dad had died alone in a strange place. God brought the circumstances into divine alignment so our broken family would be together again, even if just for a little while.

I didn't see this immediately after Dad passed away, I found myself stuck in a maze of grief over his death, anger over the short time I had with him, regret over leaving him alone and broken in his apartment years before, and hurt because God had allowed it all to happen. Satan enjoyed the two months that followed Dad's passing. I imagine the enemy sitting in the corner of whatever room I occupied, smirking and plotting his next move. Satan knew the gate of vulnerability that grief had opened allowed a way for him to come in and stay for a while.

In many ways, I blamed myself for Dad's ultimate state. Typical of many adult children of alcoholics, I thought if I had not left him alone in his dingy apartment years before, maybe he would not have ended up destitute, homeless, and alone. Satan worked on my mind and he slowly attempted to turn my abstract thoughts of regret into his twisted, condemnation. Grief, anger, remorse, and hurt were my companions for the months that followed. God was also there with me. He simply sat lovingly and patiently waiting for me to realize it.

We may not know or understand why God allows suffering to occur, but we can trust his ways are right and just. He understands suffering because of Jesus' sufferings. We are not meant to know or understand God's ways. That statement is difficult for me to swallow. I want to understand things. I want to know the why behind the action, but the faith I carry with me is what helps when I don't understand. Faith in a God who loves me through the pain. He is enough.

> *Blessed is a man who perseveres under trial; for once he has been approved, he will receive the crown of life which the Lord has promised to those who love him.*

James 1:12

Chapter 8
The Freedom of Forgiveness

...bearing with one another, and forgiving each other, whoever has a complaint against anyone; just as the Lord forgave you, so also should you.

Colossians 3:13

Forgiveness doesn't come easy. Years of hurt, betrayal, addiction, venomous words, rebellion, fights, contempt, and abandonment fog up the heart's capacity to seek true reconciliation. It gets cloudy and before you know it forgiveness seems truly impossible. The longer the resentment lingers the more difficult forgiveness becomes. I had held on to so much bitterness toward my dad, but the night in the emergency room everything came crashing down on both of us.

"Kim, your dad wants to talk to you before you leave for work," Mom said.

We had not been back from the hospital too long and I was getting ready to go to the office—one of the few days I actually showed up for work while Dad was with us.

"Morning, Dad." The memory of the night before still lingered.

"Morning, Mija," he said with a smile. "Come here and sit down real quick."

I maneuvered around the tight space of his room, stubbing my toe on the hospital bed.

"Ouch!"

He laughed. I sat.

He looked me straight in the eyes. "I'm sorry I was hateful to you earlier."

I couldn't find the words to speak in that moment. Dad never apologized for anything.

"I am just worried about your mother. I know you and Emily will be fine, it's her I worry about. I always do. I always have."

"I'll take good care of her, Dad. I always have." I smiled through teary eyes.

"I know you will. You have done so well for yourself and you are so beautiful." He smiled again.

"Thank you, Dad."

"I love you, Mija."

"I love you, too. By the way, you were already forgiven." I gave him a kiss and told him good-bye.

I meant what I said. Although it had been difficult at first, I had forgiven him for the early morning hours of the emergency room—and for many other things. That was the least I could do. He was the one grappling over his life. He didn't know how long he had to live and neither did any of us. I held my breath when my phone would ring at work or when I received a text message. I fully expected him to pass that day, but he didn't. We were able to spend one more week with him. After his last hospital visit, his mood was different. He wasn't angry at us anymore. His demeanor calmed, like he was preparing himself to go on a long trip and he wanted to savor every second. There were a few times he became agitated, but that was just him. He never liked people fussing over him and I cannot imagine what it would feel like to no longer be able to do anything independently. I cannot fathom the idea of being confined to a bed and having to wait on other people to help me up just to sit in a hot garage for a few minutes.

On the Thursday before he left this world, Leah called me.

"Mom, you might want to come home." She had been crying.

"What's wrong?"

"Papa wants to talk to you. He also asked for Grandma Rosa and Diana to come."

That was out of character for him. Not that he didn't love my grandma and aunt, it was just he didn't want a lot of people and activity around him during the weeks up to that point.

"Okay, I'm on my way."

This is it, I thought. *Today is going to be the day.* I quickly put away my papers, sent a short email, logged off my computer, locked my drawers, grabbed my purse, and walked out the door. I shook. My heart pounded in my ears. I had a long drive ahead of me and had to get myself together before I started. I decided to call Leah back.

"Hey, so how is he? What's going on?"

"He's breathing funny now. He seems really tired."

We talked during the first half of my drive. Then I needed some solitude before walking through the door. I needed to collect myself.

Just the day before, Patrick had helped Dad get a shower and a shave. Patrick took a picture of him and sent it to me at work. He looked good—as good as he could then. His eyes were deep in their sockets and his coloring had yellowed, but he smiled. It had been a good day, they told me. One of his best. His spirits were high. He and Mom had talked almost nonstop all day. He had eaten well and didn't get too tired.

I pulled my car in and left the garage door open. I knew when I walked inside, he would want to smoke. I hooked my purse on my arm and opened the car door. I could tell it had been a while since anyone had been in the garage because of the sweltering heat. I almost counted my steps to the door. I stopped, took a deep breath, and braced myself for what I might see.

I turned the corner and saw him lying in bed, mouth open, sleeping soundly, with the oxygen on and the tubes sticking up his nose.

"When did that start?" I asked Mom, pointing to the oxygen.

"About an hour ago. He's really tired today," she said. I realized for the first time how weary she looked.

Emily arrived not long after I did. Dad continued to sleep soundly. This was not something he had done in recent days. We sat at the dining room table and recounted the day in a whisper.

Ring.

I bought him a bell to ring when he needed anything and up to that day he had worn that sucker out. I pulled away from the table and walked into his room.

"Hey there, sleepyhead!"

"Hi, Mija. Can we go outside?"

"Sure we can."

We loaded up and rolled out to the garage.

His pain medication had increased so his eyes were half closed and half opened most of the time now. He would hold the cigarette between two fingers, but it only reached his mouth a few times before it burned up. He was using his blue emesis bags almost every hour, if not more. The hospice nurse told us this was to be expected. It still didn't make it any easier to see him heaving into that shiny blue bag.

That brief trip exhausted him and he only asked to go outside one more time that day. His body was finally giving way. I vowed to stay the night with him. Mom needed her rest. At that point we didn't know how much longer he would be able to hang on. We could tell his body was changing rapidly. His eyes looked hollow and they began to turn a foggy, bluish color, not the deep chocolate brown they had once been. He also didn't talk as much and only wanted small bowls of watermelon to eat. He ate and immediately needed the blue bag again.

Dad fought all night to find comfort. Restlessness overtook him as soon as I turned out the light and television and it lasted throughout the night. In between doses of sedatives and painkillers he mumbled and moaned, tossed and turned, pulled and tugged at the blankets. Rubbing his forehead in frustration, he attempted to use the urinal, but couldn't. His kidneys began to shut down.

As the sun began to peek through the blinds, I raised my head and opened one eye to see him staring over at the window. I sat up in the recliner-turned-bed and asked if he was okay.

"Yeah," he said.

"Do you want a little coffee?"

"Sure."

"It's time for your medicine too."

I shuffled into the kitchen and prepared his morning dose as the coffee brewed. I took his medicine and a half cup of cream and sugar with a dash of coffee. He took his medicine and asked one last time to smoke.

He didn't smoke his entire cigarette that morning and didn't drink all the coffee before needing the blue bag again. Then he slumped in his chair, simply tired of everything.

"Dad, can you look up at me?"

He looked up, tried to focus his eyes on me, and smiled a faint smile.

"I love you Dad. I love you so much, do you know that?"

"I do," he slurred, his mouth thick from morphine.

"You were the best father I could have ever asked for."

"I hope so, Mija."

"You were, I promise."

"I love you, Mija. Let's go in. I'm so tired."

I kissed him on the cheek and he kissed mine. I wheeled him into the house for the last time.

WHERE WAS GOD?

I don't know much about Dad's childhood, but most of what I know I learned during his last days with us. I know he went to Catholic schools. I know the nuns would slap the kids—including Dad—on the knuckles with a wooden ruler if they were mouthy. I know that his mom, and maybe the nuns too, would pour uncooked rice on the floor and make Dad kneel on it as time out for whatever trouble he had caused. I know that get-togethers at his childhood home would usually end up in a family fight. I know his dad died at a fairly young age. I know that Dad was a rebellious teen who did various illegal things. But I do know a lot about the man he had become after his youth. I know that Dad was a strong, hardworking man. I know he would have done anything in his power to protect his family, and I know Dad loved us with all his heart. In the end, that love was all I needed.

In his last days, I saw a broken man. Not just broken from the cancer, but also from his addiction. I saw how destructive the disease of cancer is but also know firsthand how destructive the disease of addiction is. As I mentioned before, I didn't have the knowledge I have now about God's love for us, but today I see God's hand in every event leading up to Dad's death.

Forgiving Dad wasn't easy. It was in the brokenness I was able to offer forgiveness to him. Instinctively, I knew he didn't have control over his addiction during the last twenty or so years of his life. Although his alcoholism and addictions had hurt me tremendously, I had to figure out a way to forgive him in order to bring peace to my aching heart. For years, the anger I had toward him for abandoning Mom bubbled on the surface, threatening to explode. I finally released the anger after the final hospital trip. The day that followed, Dad apologized to me for the first time. He showed humility and asked for grace and forgiveness. I didn't know it at the time, but I could not have given him grace if God hadn't been right there with me to show me how.

I imagine God sitting next to me that day, his hand lovingly on my shoulder, quietly urging me to open my heart to forgiveness. He knew I wouldn't understand why in that moment, but he also knew he would gradually show me. He loves me that much.

How do I know God loves me? With a dad who was an alcoholic and could leave me feeling so unlovable, how is it possible God loves me with an everlasting love? Can it really be true? Is God really a father who loves me? Yes, he is.

- *The LORD's lovingkindnesses indeed never cease, For his compassions never fail. They are new every morning; Great is Your faithfulness.* – **Lamentations 3:22-23**

- *The LORD your God is in your midst, A victorious warrior. He will exult over you with joy, He will be quiet in his love, He will rejoice over you with shouts of joy.* – **Zephaniah 3:17**

- *For I am convinced that neither death, nor life, nor angels, nor principalities, nor things present, nor things to come, nor powers, nor height, nor depth, nor any other created thing, will be able to separate us from the love of God, which is in Christ Jesus our Lord.* – **Romans 8:38-39**

- *A father of the fatherless and a judge for the widows, Is God in His holy habitation.* – **Psalm 68:5**

The word "love" is mentioned over 500 times in the Bible. It stands to reason when reading the Bible, I feel love surrounding me, even during the suffering my dad endured that restless night before he died. I felt God's loving comfort then and during the days and nights that followed.

Those last three days of Dad's life were a gift to me. The Lord loved me that much. After years of separation, God showed me in a big way the very depths of his love. He revealed that I had not only left my earthly father behind, but I also left my heavenly Father behind. I was focused only on myself. God knew I needed a wake-up call from my selfish behavior. He knew I needed to forgive so I could be forgiven. He wanted me to experience his presence and know how alive he truly is. He wanted me to realize that I should not wait until the end to allow God to fight for me. He's doing it already. The truth is we are loveable, God does love us, and we are forgiven. It's time to fight the good fight with him. Take hold of the eternal life waiting for you. Forgive the unforgiveable. Our heavenly Father already has, through sacrifice of his one and only son, Jesus Christ.

> *Fight the good fight of faith; take hold of the eternal life to which you were called, and you made the good confession in the presence of many witnesses.*

1 Timothy 6:12

Chapter 9
Finally Letting Go

The LORD is near to the brokenhearted and saves those who are crushed in spirit.

Psalm 34:18

It was solemn and quiet in my home the hours after Dad passed away. My heart ached like it was being smashed in a vice. Dad was really gone. The heavy, strained breathing had stopped. No more medicine, no more blue bag, no more smoke breaks, no more watermelon, no more television. It was all gone in what seemed like a flash.

The night Dad died I immediately felt a strange mixture of relief, horrible sadness, guilt, shame, and regret. I was relieved he wasn't in pain anymore. Isn't that what people usually say when someone dies from cancer? "Well, at least he's not in pain anymore." While that is true, as selfish human beings, we don't want anyone we love to die, especially from the "C" word. The suffering was difficult for me to watch and be a part of. During his three weeks with us, we gave him the best care he had received since he and Mom parted ways. I believe those were the best three weeks he had had in many years. Although the time was challenging, it also blessed us all.

We planned for the day, even hoped for it because of the cancerous torment, but we were not truly ready for it. Who is completely *ready* for someone to die? I mean *in fact* prepared? No one. No matter how many times the hospice nurses said, "This is normal toward the end of life," it didn't genuinely sink in. I held on to the memories of the dad I used to know before the addiction. Before the homelessness. Before the cancer. Hoping a miracle would occur. A miracle that never did.

I tucked each memory neatly inside and the door closed tight, all locked up to keep forever. Memories of him taking me to the empty high school parking lot to teach me to drive. Memories of him watching television in his bedroom sanctuary while I performed the dreaded chore of washing dishes as a teen. He would scream at the top of his lungs for me.

"Mija!"

"What?!" I would scream back.

"Come here, hurry!"

I would slump my shoulders, turn off the tap, dry my hands, and stomp all the way through the dining room, living room, down the hall, and turn the corner into my parent's room. Then it would hit me, he had passed gas and wanted me to come all the way across the house just to smell it. Typical.

"Gross, Dad! Oh my gosh! I can't believe you!" I would say as I stormed out and down the hallway. I could hear him chuckling behind me.

That was Dad. Always laughing about something or dancing into the living room. He would come sauntering down the hallway and get between the television and me and dance like James Brown while he sang "Wild Thing" or some other silly song. Mom would laugh at him and he would disappear into the kitchen, probably for watermelon.

That's the Dad I tucked into my heart. Not the one that existed after addiction took over. That's what addiction does—it steals the person deep down in the fibers of their soul and replaces them with a stranger. I know he loved us—nothing could ever stop that—but Dad's first disease, addiction, didn't take his physical life from him. Instead it took away the quality of his life. And ours.

As I sat in his makeshift hospital room in my home, I looked at his lifeless body. Those beloved memories flashed through my mind. That was all gone. Only sixty-three years had passed since Dad was born and so much of that life had been spent in pain. He loved Mom fiercely and she loved him back with just as much power, but all of the love in the world cannot cure someone of a disease.

I could not have imagined we would have ever seen Dad again after we left him five years prior, sitting alone in the rundown apartment. I certainly couldn't imagine that not only would we have found him, but he would be gone again—this time forever—just days later. The memory of those three weeks whirred past as if I sat on a train trying to focus on the blurry countryside.

Before the hospice nurse arrived to help with cleanup and preparation for the funeral home, Mom lit a candle and opened a window.

"We have to open the window to let his spirit out," she said.

I thought it must have been an old wives' tale, but I did exactly as she wanted.

After the funeral director left with Dad's body, Emily, Mom, Leah, and I were left in my starkly quiet house. It was difficult to fathom it was all over. As quickly as everything had started, it was finished. No medication to administer. No wheelchair to push out to the garage. The bed now sat empty. The house now hushed. We lit a candle for Dad.

We had agreed before Dad left us, to each take a puff of a cigarette from his last pack. I picked it up off the table and we filed to the garage. I lit the cigarette and passed it around. All but Mom commemorated Dad in this way. It was a bittersweet moment. Dad and I had spent countless hours in the garage. I didn't want to go back in the house.

I finally did go back inside that night, but the silence haunted my ears. I saw Mom and Emily in Dad's room so I went in. Mom sobbed, but we decided to go ahead and close the window and blow out the candle together. Mom, Emily, Leah, and me—all of Dad's girls—stood around the candle. In unison, we inhaled a deep breath and exhaled together until the flame disappeared into a wisp of smoke. That small dedication marked the true end for me. His flame no longer burned.

Exhaustion overwhelmed us. Nothing left to do, we said our goodnights and went our separate ways. I robotically brushed my teeth, changed my clothes, pulled back the covers, crawled into bed, and turned out the light. I lay there in the dark room, my husband's arms wrapped around my numb body. Sleep didn't come easily. Although wide awake, at one point I clearly saw Dad's image dancing around, no longer sick. I thought it was strange to have that vision come so clearly to me, but I dismissed it and tried fervently to fall asleep. We had a busy day ahead of us and the morning sun would still shine even though darkness emerged in my heart.

§

The aftermath of a death is filled with a seemingly never-ending rollercoaster of emotion. People come in and out of your home, bringing enough food to feed a small village. Any good Texan knows food is the cure for every sort of ailment, including grief. Those same well-meaning people hugged us and said things like, "he is in a better place now," the standard go-to words when someone dies. All the while we were left to handle arrangements, make phone calls, fill out paperwork, and—oh yeah—grieve. After the dust settled, all of the people and food gone, there I was standing in an empty room. The absence of the oxygen machine running, the heavy breathing, the bell ringing, the television noise, the laughter. All gone. Desolate silence.

Patrick was still there, but he typically started drinking by eight o'clock in the morning. Even at that early hour he had checked out. Mom was there, but her sadness overwhelmed her and smothered me. Everyone else had gone back to their jobs and lives. I had gone back to work, too, but I moved through my day on autopilot. My body knew what to do and where to go, so my mind just let it do its thing. I would get out of bed, wobble to the kitchen, pour a cup of coffee, and head to the garage, all without looking at the empty room on my way out. The garage had become my new home. The place Dad and I rediscovered each other again. The place we bonded. The place I forgave him. The only place I belonged.

I spent every evening there, alone with the florescent light above me, smoking way too much, mindlessly playing games on my phone or perusing social media—becoming a master of wasting time and avoiding my loved ones. I sat there allowing my tiny world to close in on itself.

I recalled each moment of the forty-three years of my life, most of which I didn't feel proud of. The guilt, regret, and grief muddled together and settled in as my latest companions.

I gradually realized that I didn't want to be like my dad, apologizing too late for the wrongs committed. I needed more than that. I needed to know I would die one day without any regrets about my past. But how? Bit by bit, I tore myself down inside, tangling in a web of mistakes and misdeeds and no longer focused on the things I had done right. Self-deprecation became a default activity while I sat in the garage.

I thought about my conversations with Dad. I recalled the day I left him in his shabby apartment to fend for himself. I tried to remember the last things I said to him and rehearsed them so I would never forget. I desperately tried to hold on to the last words he had said to me, but they escaped my grasp. I couldn't remember. I still cannot.

As the weeks ticked by, I wondered if I should continue to stay married to a man who was slowly drinking himself into the same state Dad was in all those years. I didn't know if I could or not. I didn't want to live my life that way. I didn't want to live like Mom lived for over twenty years. Fear smothered me. Fear Patrick would end up exactly like Dad. Fear I would end up hating him. The thoughts entered my mind and tucked themselves in for an extended stay until they came to the only logical conclusion. All I had to do was outline how I would tell the love of my life that our marriage was over.

§

Lost within myself—mission accomplished. Leave me alone, everyone—mission two accomplished. I am a damaged, broken, awful person and not worthy of love from anyone. Those feelings strangled me. Then something strange started happening. One night as I lay in my comfortable bed, sleeping soundly, out of nowhere at three in the morning my eyes popped open. For the next week I woke up at the exact same time. Not because of a dream. Not because I would hear a sound—the piercing silence still echoed in the house. For no apparent reason my eyelids refused to stay closed any longer, despite my exhaustion. Sneaking out of the bedroom, making the coffee as usual, and going to the garage earlier than before became my habit.

Tears would come to me at that hour. Tears I held in when people were around. I missed Dad the most in those early morning hours and I realized I had lost the entire sense of direction for my life. I had no idea what I should do or who I should be. My mind was a jumbled labyrinth I could not escape. I spent every second of every day running through the maze of my mind and coming to a dead end at every turn. The world seemed to have no color and I had no purpose. My heart had turned a charcoal lump sitting in my chest. This was a cold, desolate, lightless path I had traveled before. Depression is a well-worn road for the adult child of an alcoholic.

That week of three o'clock morning thoughts finally brought me to a turning point. A sticky web of resentment and anger controlled each thought and emotion. I resented Patrick for taking our love and drowning it in beer for the short five years of our marriage. Once I had found him again after letting him go all those years before, I expected him to be the man I had needed in my life. When the alcohol became his priority instead of spending time with me and I began to realize it, it upset me deeply. It hurt that he hadn't even noticed, even though I had never pointed out his choosing the drinking over me. The anger bubbled, just waiting for the right time to erupt.

One Sunday, after once again waking up at the magic hour, I spent most of the day in my place of solitude. It hadn't been a month since Dad had died. Patrick would frequent the garage because that is where the beer was kept. I don't recall what started the discussion that day, but I finally spewed the venomous words at him.

"I'm going to Emily's to play games. I can't sit in this house anymore."

"Oh . . . okay," he said as he sat in his usual Sunday spot.

The television blared.

I walked into the bedroom to change clothes. I braced myself, hoping he would not follow me in. I was not in the mood for a talk. He didn't and I walked out with my purse. He met me in the kitchen.

"Do you want me to come?"

"If you want to. I don't care," I said.

No, I really don't want you to come, I want to escape from you right now, I thought.

"I wish somebody still loved me," he mumbled.

"What?"

"Nothing . . . go . . . I'll see you later."

"Oh no, what did you say?" Now I wanted the discussion.

"Nothing . . . I . . . just don't . . . never mind."

"What?!"

"I just wish you still loved me."

"Why do you do that? Why do you say things like that?"

"You are just not yourself anymore. You don't want me around you at all. I don't get it."

"I never said that, now, did I?"

He had moved into the living room and back in the same spot in his chair.

"You don't have to. You stay completely away from me."

"I stay away from everyone."

"I know. I don't understand it."

"Of course you don't." This time I mumbled.

"What do you want me to do?"

"I don't know."

I didn't. I ran in the maze again; running and running, turning and turning again; still no way out. I was stuck in a corner with nowhere to go.

"I don't know, either."

"I don't know what I want anymore. I know I don't want to be stuck in this house watching television for the rest of my life. I know I don't want to die having regrets. I know I don't want to see you drink yourself into oblivion like Dad did." There it was, out on the table, just a sample of the things that had been bouncing around my mind waiting for a chance to come out.

I told him how I hated him drinking so much and no, I didn't want to be around him anymore; not like that. I told him how I wanted him to show an interest in me and doing things with me instead of staying home because that was the only safe place he could drink and not have to worry about driving anywhere. I was sick of buying beer and being alone in my house with my husband. I told him I didn't feel like I was a wife and he wasn't a husband anymore. I was done.

The yelling over, we both sat in the same places and positions for what seemed like hours before he broke the silence.

"Okay, well, I'll stop then."

"Okay."

That was it. He would just stop. He had drunk pretty much his entire adult life and just like that, he will stop. This I had to see. I had huge doubts about it. I knew he was just trying to pacify the situation. He wanted to put a piece of chewed up gum on a leaking ship. Even though I doubted his motives, I still tried to show support in the coming days. I chalked up the feelings I had to grief and nothing more.

Days before, I decided to go see a therapist. I searched through my insurance and called several places, but either they didn't have an appointment available for new patients for months out or they never called me back. Only one of the many I left messages for called me back within an hour.

"Kimberly?" a sweet voice said after I reluctantly pushed the green answer button on the phone sitting at my desk at work.

"This is she," I said.

"This is Polly. You left me a message?"

I looked down the list I had used to make calls that morning.

"Oh, yes. Thank you for calling me back. I was wondering if I could make an appointment to come see you this Friday. After five o'clock if possible."

There was silence from the other end.

"Hmm . . . let me look here."

I knew what was coming. I knew she wouldn't have anything available for probably a year.

"How about noon this Friday? I can do that. I stop taking appointments at four o'clock so I can spend time with my family."

I considered it for a moment.

"I'm sorry, I can't come in the middle of the day. I work kinda far from where you are." I looked back at my list; she was the last one that I hadn't marked a big X through.

"I'm so sorry, I am pretty booked up. I tell you what, I will go ahead and put your name down in that spot and mark it as 'possible'. If you can't make it or if you find someone else that can fit into your schedule better, just call me back. How does that sound?"

"That sounds good." Her voice was soothing and nice. Most of the others I had already talked to didn't have the warmness she did. She sounded like someone I could be friends with.

"Okay, done. You just let me know, okay?"

"Okay. Thank you."

I pressed end on my phone and laid it on my desk. I sat there for a few minutes and thought about how I could possibly go see her. For some reason, I knew I needed to talk to her. I decided to wait until the next day and if I didn't find anyone else, I would call her back and figure out a way to fit it into my work schedule.

The next day came and I continuously checked my phone because I was afraid I had missed a call from another therapist that miraculously found an open slot for me, maybe even Polly. Nothing. The phone sat on my desk and stared back at me blankly. I decided if I hadn't heard from anyone after I returned from lunch, I would call Polly and work the noon appointment into my schedule. I went to lunch and came back to my desk.

I felt on the verge of tears every minute that passed. It was all I could do to hold it together while I was at work. I had so much responsibility and so many people depended on me. I couldn't fall apart, but that's exactly what I wanted to do. I actually wanted to crack so I could spend a few days away from everything and everyone in some solitude. I desperately wanted to find peace, but didn't know where or how to find it.

I picked up my phone and found Polly's number in the list. I pressed her name and waited.

"This is Polly."

"Um . . . hi . . . this is, um . . . Kimberly. I spoke to you yesterday."

"Oh, hi, Kimberly!" Wow, how can someone, especially a therapist, be so darned happy?

"Um . . . I think . . . well . . . I'll be there at noon on Friday if you still have me penciled in."

"Oh, that's great! Yes, I have you down."

I gave her my email address and we ended the call. My heart raced and I didn't know why. I was not my normal, calm self. I wouldn't call it excitement, but I did find some relief. I had been to a therapist before, but my experience was not that great. I didn't want to take pills in order to find peace. I couldn't be medicated to get over my grief and anger. I had talked to my family, but they were biased. They could really only see my side of the matter. The more they talked, the deeper I went into the maze in my mind. I felt like I was truly losing it.

I didn't realize Polly was a Christian therapist. I still believed in God and wasn't angry with him, I just didn't regard him much at all. Not until I sat down with Polly the first time. After we talked that day, I felt some hope, but I was still jumbled in my own thoughts. She recommended the book *The Power of a Praying Wife* by Stormie Omartian, and also suggested I go to a group that focused on families of alcoholics. I didn't want to talk to anyone else. I didn't want to air my dirty laundry out to complete strangers. I folded up the brochure she gave me, stuck it in my purse, and made my next appointment. I secretly wished she would have said something like, "I really think you should be committed, I'll draw up the paperwork right now and call an escort for you." When that didn't happen, I remember feeling the pang of disappointment. Didn't she think I was crazy? I know I felt that way. Instead she asked if we could pray. I was a little taken aback. I hadn't really prayed since the early morning hours with an open Bible as Dad lay in the hospital bed. Other than that, prayer was a distant memory of my younger years.

Her prayer was simple, but it brought me to tears. God spoke through her then and he continued to do so the entire time I saw her. Each session ended in a prayer. God knocked on my heart, but I refused to go to the door. I just sat in the corner, rocking back and forth in the darkness of my mind.

Patrick stopped drinking the day after the big eruption. He seemed to be doing fine and we had made up, but uncertainty haunted me. I had seen this so many times before with several people in my life's history, especially with Dad. My gut told me it was only temporary.

Our next two weeks were pretty good. Patrick wasn't drinking, but I still was not present in the marriage. I felt a sense of unsettledness and couldn't figure out why initially. I thought the doubts I had about Patrick giving up the beer caused the restlessness.

"You know, I bet that in a few months, I will be able to have a beer at dinner and be okay, don't you?" Patrick casually asked one afternoon.

"Um . . . no . . . I don't think that. You are an alcoholic."

"There are a lot of people that can do that you know."

"Dad always said, 'I can't even go into a bar without wanting a drink.' That was before he started drinking again, of course."

"I know, but maybe I can."

That did it for me. I knew in that moment he already thought of how he would be able to drink something—anything—again. Only two and a half weeks after the venom of anger spewed in our living room, he was still blind to it. He still couldn't see that he was an alcoholic that couldn't drink because one drink turned into twenty. It was a lost cause. I closed up again and retreated inside myself where I felt more at home than I did in my marriage. I drifted back into the darkness that had become my best friend, feeling sorry for myself and finding refuge in the garage, away from real life.

The next morning, you guessed it, at three o'clock, my eyelids sprang open and my back ached. I turned over and slipped out of bed, hoping I wouldn't be discovered. Patrick was generally a light sleeper. If he knew I had left the bed, he kept quiet. I was good with that. I slowly turned the doorknob and quietly closed the door behind me. Barely seeing through the darkness of the living room, I felt my way to click on the light. I squinted as I walked to the coffee pot and I began my morning ritual of filling the pot with grounds and water to make the magic elixir that would help my eyes focus on the day ahead.

I poured my coffee, grabbed my phone, and walked out to the garage. I sat there sipping on my favorite drink and wondering why three was the mysterious number. Why was that the time every single morning that my body was stirred out of a deep sleep? I perused social media on my phone and found picture after picture on my favorite app, Pinterest, which reminded me of Dad. I looked at endless posts that spoke about death of a loved one. I pinned and pinned, wasting the early morning hours like I did every other minute of the day.

Suddenly, something stopped my scrolling. A Bible verse caught my attention. My eyes scanned the words, *"The Lord is near to the brokenhearted, and saves those who are crushed in spirit"* Psalm 34:18.

I was crushed in spirit.

I was brokenhearted.

Did that mean God was close to me, too?

I shook the thought away. How could God be close to me? I had abandoned Dad when he needed his family the most, I was an adulteress, and I hadn't been close to him in a very long time. I didn't deserve his closeness anymore. I was too far gone.

The next morning, same time, I slithered out of bed and repeated the same routine. Again, I sat in the garage and looked through the social media feed of the day. I laid my phone down and sipped on my coffee. Then, out of nowhere, I thought about my Bible. The one I had ordered over a year before after watching a television show about heaven and hell. It had occurred to me then that I didn't own a Bible anymore, so I ordered one. I sat there for a moment and tried to recall where I had put it. I went inside to my study and clicked on the light. I scanned the room and spotted it on the table with the printer. I walked over and picked it up. I lifted it to the light and blew at the cover—dust flew. I lifted my hand and wiped the remaining layer off the top of the book. Satisfied, I stuck it under my arm and walked back to the garage.

I sat in the chair and laid the daily Scripture reading and devotional Bible by Max Lucado on my lap. Taking another sip of coffee, I turned the pages to find that day's date. I read the words carefully.

"Help me, O LORD my God; Save me according to Your lovingkindness." I read and re-read the words from Psalm 109:26 over and over again. I needed to be saved from the pit of my life. I had forgotten how to ask for help. God helped me see. A glimmer of light began to peek into my darkness. I continued to read.

"Let them curse, but you bless" (Psalm 109:28a). I re-read that line and replaced "them" with "me."

"Let me curse, but you bless me." Yes. I did curse myself. I had been doing so since Dad died. Something inside me slowly began to change, like the earth shifting under the rumble of an aftershock.

"For he stands at the right hand of the needy, to save him from those who judge his soul" (Psalm 109:31).

It occurred to me that I had been my biggest accuser. Not one person in my life had accused me of anything. I had been the one torturing myself for the past month and a half. The epiphany struck me and in that moment the sun slowly began to peek through the dark clouds within. I was still confused about what to do with my marriage, but I felt a nudge. God wanted me to talk to him. I also felt the need to continue seeing Polly because she was a Christian, and trained to help people like me, the way God wanted me to be helped.

The feeling that Patrick needed to go still remained. I didn't want to hurt him—not again— but I couldn't continue to live knowing he was one sip away from going right back to the way he was. An alcoholic cannot have even one drink. That one drink turns into ten or twenty. Then the mood changes, the discontentedness sets in, sometimes depression follows, withdrawal occurs. No—a true alcoholic cannot have even one taste.

I knew by his comment he wasn't committed to stop drinking and in that moment, I wasn't committed to loving him through it.

§

The Bible tells us that God hates divorce. I battled over the next few days with extreme guilt and shame for having been married three times. I struggled with the dishonor of having been an adulterous woman during my second marriage. I combated the guilt of abandoning Dad when I felt like he needed me the most. I slowly realized that I had contributed to Patrick's disease. I hadn't caused Patrick to be an alcoholic, but I enabled it. All of these feelings manifested themselves like storm clouds slowly building right before a tornado spawns. They swirled around, slowly building momentum, waiting for the opportune moment to strike.

God continued to wake me at the same time every morning. He knew, I began to realize, that was the only time of day where I could completely focus on him. He taught me how to talk to him again. He guided me through the words of the Bible. Isaiah 50:4b told me, *"He awakens me every morning, he awakens my ear to listen as a disciple."* God, the teacher, and me, the student. I had forgotten how to listen to him. I had forgotten how to pray to him. I had forgotten how to just be.

That morning, I prayed with tears streaming down my face. I begged him to tell me what to do.

"God, if you are listening, please, I don't know what to do. I feel like I am completely broken in half. I don't want Patrick here, but I don't have the strength to tell him. There is so much I know you need from me and I don't know how to give it. Do you want me to tell him to leave? That is what is in my heart, but it is breaking because of it. I beg you to show me the way, God. I need you now more than I ever have. I need your help, God! Please, give me strength."

The awkward, broken prayer hung in the quiet of the garage. God knew how broken I was. He knew how much I needed him. That is why he tugged at my heart to get the Bible only days before. He had things to tell me and I needed to listen. As I finished my prayer,

I heard the door to the garage open and close. My heart sank. Patrick walked up and sat in a chair across from me.

Our words were harsh.

"Do you want me here?" he asked.

"I don't know," I said.

"What does that mean?"

"It means I don't know."

"Do you love me anymore?"

"I don't know."

We sat in silence for a few moments.

"Just tell me what you want me to do," he said.

I sat still, staring at the floor.

"I need to know what you want from me," he said.

"I think you need to leave." I couldn't look at him. I sat, emotionless. It was like the words came from someone else's mouth.

"Wow," he said.

"I'm sorry, I don't love you the way a wife should love you right now. I think it would be best if you left."

"Just like that? You just want me to leave, just like that?"

"You know this is not easy for me."

He slowly rose from his chair and went in the house, slamming the door behind him. I closed my eyes and whispered to God, "I hope I'm doing the right thing."

I got up and went inside. Patrick was in the bedroom furiously packing a suitcase.

"I would like you to give me the garage door opener and your key to the house please."

He looked at me with contempt.

"What do you think I'm going to do?"

"Nothing, I just think it would be best."

"Fine." He took his key off the ring and I walked out of the room.

The next couple of days were filled with relief and sadness mixed with regret and longing. I didn't like coming home and Patrick not being there, but I somehow knew it had to be that way. I knew he had to realize I no longer wanted to live my life in the cycle of addiction. I had my own issues to deal with and my faith was one of those issues.

My marriage was broken, but my relationship with God was too. I needed to mend my relationship with God first. He had gently tugged at my heart for a while. He wanted me to draw close to him but I pushed his promptings aside for far too long. My life became a dark, self-centered world. I had looked to the wrong places and things for peace.

Patrick gave me the space I told him I needed. He only texted me at night to say he loved me. The first night, I didn't text back. The next night he sent me an email, but I didn't respond to it either. I needed complete separation from him. I didn't know for how long. Each hour that passed, I became more confused. I still ran around the maze and couldn't figure out my next steps.

Before I told Patrick to leave, I spoke with my family daily. They knew about the struggles I experienced. I dragged them into my maze and they ran around in there with me. I led the life of a co-dependent. Although I professed my strength and self-reliance, I fell back into being needy quickly. After Patrick left, I turned to God and God alone. I wish I had turned to him sooner.

Two days later, Leah called me at work.

"Do you mind if Patrick comes to the house and picks up some clothes?" she asked.

"Of course not. Today?"

"No, tomorrow."

"Did he call you? What did he say?"

"He just texted and asked me to tell Nana and see if you would be okay with it."

My heart immediately raced in my chest. The whole day seemed like a dream; actually the events of the past two months seemed like a dream. I didn't envision my life being like this. Three times married and facing being alone again. I thought once Patrick and I reunited after over twenty years apart, we would live happily ever after. This was my plan. This was how things were supposed to work out. Another divorce was not in the plan.

I went to Polly's that day. I'm sure she saw the confusion on my face as I sat down.

"So, what's been going on? How was last week?" she asked.

"Patrick is gone."

"Oh. So you asked him to leave?"

"Yes."

"How do you feel about that now?"

"I don't know."

The tears flowed down my cheeks. I dropped my face into my hands and she let me cry for as long as I needed to.

I spilled everything I had bottled up for the past twenty years— the guilt over Dad, the adultery, the divorces, and the DUI; how I felt unloved and unwanted, how I missed God but didn't know how to get right with him again.

It felt good to let it all out. Talking with a good, Christian woman is exactly what I needed. After the hour session, she prayed with me and I left.

I walked out to my car, opened the door and got in. I sat there and stared out the windshield into nothingness, wondering where I would be in five years. Wondering where I would be in one year. I even wondered where I would be the next week.

My commute is my thinking time. During the forty-five minute drive, I can let my thoughts float around and usually by the time I arrive, I am prepped for the day. I know what I will say at a meeting or how to complete each task efficiently. Work I am very good at, marriage, as it turned out, not so much. That thought floated up to the surface as I arrived in the bank parking lot. That was it—that was the golden key—marriage is just not something I could do. It wasn't my forte. All this time, I could have just remained single and alone and I would have been fine. No one would have gotten hurt, including me.

I thought about this more on my drive home that night. How could I be so good at leading people in a company, but be horrible with one person? I decided to go to my bedroom after dinner and pray and meditate on all of this. I felt an urgency to seek God and no one else through my inner struggle. I had done enough talking to other people.

I ate dinner, helped put away dishes and food, grabbed my Bible and closed the bedroom door behind me.

§

Alone in the dark, I lay in the bed I had shared with my husband for the last five years. At night his leg would prop up on the backs of my legs as I slept on my stomach. Sometimes only our feet would touch. Rarely would we not touch at all. That night marked three complete days since Patrick moved out. I knew he would be coming back home the next day long enough to grab some clothes. The rest, I assumed, would be sorted out later. But for now, I lay in the bed, closed my eyes, centered myself, and prepared for a long conversation with God. The only sound in the room came from my breathing. I became completely still.

I felt God in the room. The hairs on my arms stood on end. I felt a sinking feeling like catching myself right before falling off a cliff. I opened my eyes for a brief moment and closed them again. I spoke.

"God, I know you are here." My heart raced. "I am lost and so broken. I can't do this anymore. I've been trying to do it, but I just can't." Tears rolled down the sides of my face into my ears.

I felt the urge to turn over and flick on the light. The brightness hurt my eyes, but I needed to go back to the Scripture I had read that morning. I grabbed my Bible and turned to Ephesians 2:5: " . . . *even when we were dead in our transgressions, made us alive together with Christ (by grace you have been saved)."*

I didn't immediately understand the words that morning and even reading it a second time, it still didn't make complete sense. I felt God telling me I had already been forgiven for all of it.

Dear Lord, please forgive me. Forgive me for being so selfish, forgive me for turning away from you, just please forgive me for everything. Please, I need you in my heart again. I need you in my life again.

A feeling of relief washed over me as the tears flowed down my cheeks. In that moment it all became clear. Christ died for me. He carried the burden of my sins for me. He sacrificed his life on the cross for me. He did this so I would have the grace and the mercy I so desperately sought. I had searched my entire life for love and acceptance. In that moment I found what had been missing for so many years. I picked up my Bible again and read more: " . . . *remember that you were at that time separate from Christ, excluded from the commonwealth of Israel, and strangers to the covenants of promise, having no hope and without God in the world. But now in Christ Jesus you who formerly were far off have been brought near by the blood of Christ"* Ephesians 2:12-13.

"Thank you, heavenly Father. Thank you for saving me and giving me hope again." I laughed through my tears.

I continued to read and re-read the words until I felt them intimately. I sensed God smiling. I slept through the night and only my alarm going off at five o'clock woke me. I lay there for a few minutes thanking him for the rest and for saving me from myself.

Feeling so much lighter from days of heavy darkness, I saw things in a new way. The world around me no longer appeared bleak and stormy; the sun shone in my life again. The maze in my mind disappeared. God had led me out of the labyrinth. I was refreshed and ready to face whatever the day held.

As I sat in the garage and took the first sip of the steaming coffee, I picked up the Bible and turned to Ephesians 4:22: " . . . *that, in reference to your former manner of life, you lay aside the old self, which is being corrupted in accordance with the lusts of deceit."*

I had never considered myself as being evil, but this Scripture struck me. I know God told me to leave the old behind and start as new. The night before had changed my heart, but if I didn't change my actions along with my heart, then I wasn't truly changed at all. I had some work to do. I began to write down things I knew needed to change.

Time had turned me into a bitter person. Abuse, addiction, and broken marriages had created someone who focused merely on me and nobody else. People would talk to me and I was so self-consumed, I would not hear a word they said. Controlling the people and events in my life was something I simply had to do. I told others and myself that my experiences had created the strong woman I had become, but in reality I was a selfish, overbearing woman.

I arrived home from work that night and walked into the bedroom to change clothes. Fridays at work always seemed like the longest day of the week. I opened the door and flipped the light switch. I immediately noticed Patrick had been to the house and his pillow was missing from his side of the bed. My heart did a flip in my chest. I went to his dresser and opened the drawers. I suppose I had expected he would have emptied them completely, but some of his socks, T-shirts, and sleep pants still lay in their respective spots.

I walked into the bathroom to shed the layers of clothes and exhaustion from the day and lying by the sink was a note: *I'll be praying for both of us – I love you Kim.*

I dropped it back onto the counter and finished changing into comfortable clothes. I had vowed earlier in the day to eat dinner and go straight to meditation and prayer. I wanted to hear from God again. I needed guidance. My heart ached to tell Patrick to come back home, but remained torn about what to do. God had started me on my healing journey, but Satan still sat in the corner, reminding me of the past. That is how the enemy works; he finds my weaknesses and consistently shifts them to the forefront of my brain, reminding me of dark places. In the midst of this struggle I wanted to hear more from God, so I did as I had promised and began to seek him.

I pushed away the negative thoughts and focused on the Scripture I read that morning. Then I received a text message. Patrick wanted to talk, if I didn't mind too much. I sat on the edge of the bed and stared at the blinking cursor on the screen. I didn't know what to say back. I immediately closed my eyes and sat in the quiet.

Be still and know that I am God. I felt the words seep in.

I opened my Bible to that day's reading. I highlighted several verses that touched me that morning. My eyes were drawn to Ephesians 4:27: " . . . *and do not give the devil an opportunity.*"

I repeated those words softly to myself.

"Help me, God. What are you trying to tell me?"

Be still.

"Should I text him back, Lord?"

Do not give the devil an opportunity.

"I just don't know what to do. I love him, you know I do, I give it to you. I let go of all of it. I want you to control it all, Lord."

The phone trilled. *If you don't want to talk, I understand. Just know that I love you and I miss you. I'm still praying for us.*

Patrick was not one to pray or to talk about praying. Neither of us had been. We both believed God existed, but that was it. We hadn't had a relationship with God the first time we were together and not much had changed after we reunited. We had several discussions about religion and we both agreed that religion—organized religion—had interfered with the truth of God's word. Christianity seemed to be lost in the various religious rules and guidelines and both of us had experiences in different churches where hypocrisy was rampant: Christians saying one thing, but doing the complete opposite.

Things were shifting, though. Patrick prayed for us. Maybe he was praying for help like I was. *Had he had an experience like mine?* I wondered as I sat in the dark room. *No way, that would be too weird.* In that moment, I felt that thing in my heart again, the flutter like going down a sharp hill in a fast moving car. I immediately knew what I needed to do.

I reached for my phone and opened the text message screen. I told Patrick that I did want to talk. He immediately called me. We talked for over three hours that night and agreed to meet the next day. He told me he had reached out for help with his alcoholism. He was finally ready. God showed up again, only this time instead of guiding Dad home, he was there to help our marriage begin again.

WHERE WAS GOD?

So if God hates divorce, why would he whisper to my heart to tell my husband to leave? Why would God advise me to separate from Patrick? God knew both of us had steered our lives in a direction we thought was right, but he knew better. Remember, he is an omniscient God. I imagine him watching over us, making attempts to guide our paths straight, and all the while we get in his way. I imagine the frustration like that of an earthly father, shaking his head back and forth in disappointment at our repeated mistakes.

Since he is loving and merciful, he speaks softly to our hearts. He urges us to listen. Sometimes he urges in big ways and sometimes it is a whisper, but his persistence is driven by pure love.

I had no control growing up with an alcoholic father. As I grew into an adult, I had a compulsive need to be in control of every other situation in my life. The older I became, the deeper the need imbedded itself within me. This is common for someone raised in such a dysfunctional home. Controlling people, situations, outcomes, and finances is how I dealt with a soul in chaos. After Dad's death, I felt as though I ran around in a maze and couldn't escape. I had uncertainty about every aspect of life and who I had become. I had a clouded vision of true love and God's character as a father. I searched in the early morning hours for answers. I found them in the Bible.

God urged me to blow the dust off a Bible I hadn't touched in years and when I did, I found what I needed. His love surrounded me in those hours and has continued to surround me every single day since. This is because God never left. Through the pain, struggles, divorces, bad decisions, hurt, guilt, regret, and grief, God was there. God didn't move away from me, I moved away from him.

Once I let go of my own wants and let God take care of my needs, I found peace. Finally, the silence was not so loud. Finally, the pain became easier to bear. Finally, I felt true love. Letting go and letting God do his work in my life and in the life of my husband is when things began to move down the path it should have been on from the start.

I realized all the control I thought I had over our lives was not only exhausting, it was an illusion. I surrendered all to the Lord my God.

- I surrendered my bitterness toward Dad to him. If Jesus can bear the sins of the world so that we may be forgiven, then how can I not forgive those who have hurt me? (Matthew 6:14)

- I surrendered my will to him. I realized the purpose for my life was not my will but that of my Father God. The years of trying to live according to my plan hadn't worked out so well, so what did I have to lose by trusting in God's will for me? (Galatians 2:20)

- I surrendered my brokenness, hurt, guilt, regret, and suffering to him. I know he cares for me and I know this life is temporary. One day the brokenness, hurt, guilt, regret, and suffering of this world will be no more and he will wipe away all of my tears. (Revelation 21:4)

The night I surrendered to God is when I began to live again. He freed me to live in pure joy of his love, comfort, and promises. I acknowledged my transgressions, repented of my sins, and he has been faithful and just to forgive them all (1 John 1:9). I am free from the dark places of addiction for the first time in my life and for that I am eternally grateful.

Understand this, co-dependency is an addiction in and of itself. As a result of what we are accustomed to growing up, we believe we can control others' behavior. We see a family member contributing to an addiction and we begin to believe that is normal. Patrick has an addiction to alcohol and my drug of choice is control. I enabled his addiction by trying to control how much he drank. He enabled mine by allowing me to attempt to control how much he drank. Thankfully, this perpetual cycle has ended in two broken people learning not to depend upon each other, but to be fully dependent upon God.

God saved our marriage and he saved both of us. We are two new people—separately and as one.

> *Therefore if anyone is in Christ, he is a new creature; the old things passed away; behold, new things have come.*

2 Corinthians 5:17

Epilogue

Let your light shine before men in such a way that they may see your good works, and glorify your Father who is in heaven.

Matthew 5:16

These pages of my story have already been written and the ending is decided. Looking back, I would never have guessed my life would be the way it is today. I would never have guessed I would have dedicated my life and work to God. I did not grow up attending church on a regular basis. I was taught to believe in God, but didn't learn much about his character. I didn't have an intimate relationship with him until the darkness drove me to turn over the control I thought I had to the one who is truly in control. I didn't realize it at the time, but things were about to shift in a profound way.

Patrick came back home where he belonged and we are still moving through the healing process, one day at a time. Our communication has changed and we actually talk to each other about our feelings. That is something we should have done long before the lines of interaction shut down. I learned Patrick had a profound moment with God the day I asked him to leave. He was driving and had to pull over and completely stop. All he had to do was be still. God did the rest.

Things happen in the stillness. When the noise of a busy day shuts off and I am left with only the sound of my own breathing, God meets me there. He wraps his arms around me and tells me everything is going to be okay. He will never leave me or forsake me. The sky doesn't break open, angels don't sing, I don't see anyone's face, and I don't hear a grand booming voice speaking down from heaven, but I know he is there. I feel his presence and I have the comfort I need every time. He guides my life, now that I have abandoned my own will and replaced it with his.

I still miss my dad, but I miss him in a different way. I know the battle he fought in his last days and hours has been won. I know he is with his heavenly Father. I know God's plans are so much bigger than mine and they are perfect. He has stitched the days and years of my life into a comforting quilt of grace, mercy, and love. He plucked Dad from his darkness and placed him in the light of his family again. God wanted Dad to know how loved he was no matter what circumstances he had been in before.

I'm not old, but I am not a spring chicken anymore, as Nanny used to say. In my mind, sometimes I am still in my twenties with two babies, wishing the years would hurry up and pass by. Some days I am in my thirties with my dreams of becoming an author fresh and new. Most days I am grateful I managed to survive without too many scars on my heart—scars that once were fresh and purple, but are now fading with time. Difficult things happen to everyone, but it is how we respond to them that matters.

I was saved by the blood of Jesus Christ in my late twenties because I was desperate to find peace. I asked him to come into my heart, but I didn't completely understand the meaning behind my commitment. Instead I behaved like the chosen people of Israel. I talked to God when I needed him, but when everything moved the way I thought it was supposed to move, I ignored him. I thought God had led me to the Promised Land when Patrick and I reunited; instead I still wandered the desert, thirsty and hungry for something I couldn't even name.

Then God showed up in a huge way. He brought Dad back to me—to us—although not for long. He gave us the gift of reconciliation, forgiveness, and love. I turned away from God for so many years because I thought he was angry with me. He decided I needed something big to get my attention. Dad was the messenger and having him die in the warmth and comfort of a loving home and soft bed surrounded by those he loved was the most wonderful gift I could have been given.

Grief does unbelievable things to a human's psyche. I had to succumb to complete darkness before God could shine his light on me completely. I had to move out of the way so he could do the work he had come to do. In my mind's eye I can see Jesus walking with me, sometimes carrying me through the years.

Patrick and I have a marriage now I have always wanted to have. A marriage that is full of love, respect, compassion, support, and all of it without conditions. We both chose love and we continue to choose love each and every day. We are committed now in a way we have never experienced before. God has taught us that a husband should love his wife just as Christ loved the church, enough to lay down his life for her (Ephesians 5:25). I truly believe Patrick would do that for me. His love is unconditional and his support is unending.

God had a lot of work to do with both of us. If he can create the world and everything in it in seven short days, then it is no wonder he was able to show us the way to healing each other and our marriage in only four days apart. Miracles actually do happen. I've seen it and I have lived it. God is fully alive and working in my life. All I had to do was just be still and seek him. That is all he wants. He wants a relationship with me. He wants a relationship with you. Not a superficial relationship where I send him wishes and they are granted to me like a genie. No. He wants me to seek him in everything I do and love him with all my heart, all my soul, and all my mind (Luke 10:27). He wants me not to seek other idols like money, success, and prestige, but to seek him and him alone.

Christianity is not religion and religion is not Christianity. Going to a specific church is not going to save my soul from an eternity filled with fire and torture. Turning my heart and life over to Jesus and making him Lord of my life is what has saved me. Christ burdened himself with my sins and suffered and died on the cross on Calvary for me (1 Peter 2:24). If he can do that so I may be forgiven of my sins, how could I fail to accept forgiveness and then extend it to others?

I am a sinner. I was born that way, but I know I am forgiven because I asked for it. I am forgiven because of Jesus. I have repented of my past and have promised not to go down the same path I went down before. God leads me every day because each morning his mercies are new (Lamentations 3:23) and I turn that day over to him. Every. Single. Morning. I have moved out of his way and replaced my will with his. I do still find myself trying to take the reins again, it's in my nature and I am not perfect, but then I hear that small voice telling me to let go and be still.

I remain on my journey of healing, but those old wounds that broke open when Dad died are slowly closing back up again. Jesus had scars because of the wounds he bore for us. He dwelt with the sinners and the broken as he walked with his people, so I have faith and knowledge that he walks with me, too. My road to recovery is one that I walk daily. Sometimes he walks in front of me leading the way, sometimes he walks beside me with his arms wrapped around me, and sometimes he carries me through.

My recovery is based on biblical teachings, but I also find support with others who face similar challenges due to the addictions of loved ones. Every week I meet with them and we confide in each other because we understand each other. They get it. They understand.

Patrick and I joined a warm and welcoming church a month after our recovery began. God wants us to fellowship with others and a good Bible teaching church is a great place to do it. We have both discovered that church is more than just an hour of entertainment on Sunday. Here we learn about the Bible, praise God, serve others, and make friends to lean on in good times and times of trouble. Fellowship with other believers in Jesus equips us for our healing journey.

Jesus told his disciples, *"I am the Light of the world; he who follows Me will not walk in the darkness, but will have the Light of life"* (John 8:12b). The darkness that once consumed me has been overcome by his light. It's time for me to share the beauty of his radiance with the world.

> *You are the light of the world. A city set on a hill cannot be hidden; nor does anyone light a lamp and put it under a basket, but on the lampstand, and it gives light to all who are in the house. Let your light shine before men in such a way that they may see your good works, and glorify your Father who is in heaven.*

Matthew 5:14–16

WHERE DO I GO FROM HERE?

After walking with me through my journey, my prayer is that you have seen addiction as a disease, the patterns we repeat as adult children of alcoholics, and how to overcome them. I pray you will continue on your own journey of recovery and begin to break the cycle. I pray you know you are not alone in your struggles. I am there with you and, most importantly, God has been and will continue to be with you through it all.

Jesus loves you extremely. God, as your loving Father, desires a relationship with you. The first step on your journey into recovery is to know you are forgiven and loved! Now that you have read my story and know how God is forever faithful through my life, you can discover how he is faithful in yours as well. A great place to start is by reading the book of John in the New Testament. Pick any version of the Bible you would like. I have used the New American Standard

Bible (NASB) as my primary reference in *Three Weeks to Forgiveness: God's Redemption in the Dark Places of Addiction.*

After reading, I pray you will embrace God's gracious spirit, merciful care, and unfailing love. You don't have to wait. He wants you to come as you are. Right now. This moment. Begin your recovery journey with God as your loving Father. When you are ready, say this simple prayer. Be still and know he is the God who loves you.

Heavenly Father,

I come to you today and ask for forgiveness for my sins. Forgive me for my transgressions against you. I pray you will come into my heart, Jesus, and save me from my sins. As Romans 10:9 says, "...that if you confess with your mouth Jesus as Lord, and believe in your heart that God raised Him from the dead, you will be saved." I believe this to be true. I ask you to be the Lord of my life. Help and guide me through my recovery from my past. Thank you for loving me.

In Jesus' Precious Name,

Amen!

If you said this simple prayer, you have been saved by grace through faith in Jesus Christ. It is important to find a Bible-teaching church so you can fellowship with others and learn more about God the Father, who cares deeply for you.

May God bless you and keep you in your journey.

Resources

Celebrate Recovery - Biblically based recovery program.

Al-anon Family Groups - Friends and families of problem drinkers find understanding and support at Al-Anon and Alateen meetings.

Nar-anon Family Groups - 12 step program for friends and families of addicts.

Alcoholics Anonymous - 12 step program for alcoholics.

Narcotics Anonymous - 12 step program for addicts.

Victims of Physical Abuse - If you feel as though you might be a victim of domestic abuse or may be fearful of your safety, call the National Domestic Abuse Hotline for help.

Your safety is of utmost importance. Computer use can be monitored and it is _impossible_ to completely clear from your computer. If you are afraid your Internet searches could be monitored, _CALL don't search or click on the Internet_.

You are not alone!

The National Domestic Abuse Hotline

"Operating around the clock, seven days a week, confidential and free of cost, the National Domestic Violence Hotline provides lifesaving tools and immediate support to enable victims to find safety and live lives free of abuse. Callers to The Hotline at **1-800-799-SAFE (7233)** can expect highly trained, experienced advocates to offer compassionate support, crisis intervention information and referral services in over 170 languages. Visitors to this site can find information about domestic violence, safety planning, local resources and ways to support the organization." Source: http://www.thehotline.org/about-us

Connect with the Author

Email: info@kimberlydewberry.com

Website: www.kimberlydewberry.com

Twitter: https://twitter.com/Dewberry_Author/

Facebook: https://www.facebook.com/kimberlydewberryauthor/

Pinterest: https://www.pinterest.com/dewberry5045/

Instagram: https://www.instagram.com/dewberryauthor/

Made in the USA
Monee, IL
28 June 2024

60890703R00090